Guardians of the Avenue:

African-American Officers with the Indianapolis Police Department

By Patrick R. Pearsey
2017

Introduction

This is a general history of the contributions and achievements of African-American officers of the Indianapolis Police Department, which existed from 1854-2006. It became known as the Indianapolis Metropolitan Police Department in January 2006 after merging with the Marion County Sheriff Department.

The chief resource for this project are the on line archives of the *Indianapolis Recorder*, the newspaper that served the African-American community of Indianapolis since the 1897. They have their archives available on the internet, covering the years 1899-2005. The Recorder paid particular attention to crime reporting and hence, their issues have excellent accounts of the African-American officers of the Indianapolis Police Department. Unless otherwise noted, photographs in this history came from the Recorder. Numerous other sources came from the archives of *The Indianapolis News* and *The Indianapolis Star*.

Patrick Pearsey, IMPD Archivist

The city of Indianapolis, founded in 1822, did not have an established police force until September of 1854, when Mayor James McCready appointed 14 men to serve that purpose.   It went through major growing pains, being disbanded in 1855 and 1856.   In May 1857, another police force of 7 men lead by Captain A.D. Rose, was founded.

Due to the rising cost of housing city prisoners in the county jail (still a problem today), it was decided in 1868 to build the department a station house, which would include a jail.   A vacant lot on South Alabama Street at Pearl Street (more of an alley), was chosen for the site.   Work was completed in the fall of 1870 at a cost of $9,500.[1]

In 1873, Democrats took control of Indianapolis politics for the only time in 7 election terms.   This caused all but three of the police officers to resign.   The police force was reorganized on May 20, 1873. One of the new men hired was a turnkey (who worked in the jail) named Conrad Burley, described as "colored". He lasted 3

---

[1] "Indianapolis Police Department 2006", .14

months and was assigned to take care of prisoners in the police department jail. While he should be considered a police officer, as a turnkey, he never patrolled the streets or made arrests.

May 21, 1873:

POLICE REORGANIZED
"Contrary to general expectation the Police Board yesterday placed in the hands of Chief Thompson the list of their appointees, which were announced at roll call last evening. The position of the force is as follows:

A. P. Hipwell and Conrad Barley, (colored), station house police.[2]

July 1, 1873:

"The prisoners in the station house last night attempted to overpower Conrad Burley, the colored policeman, while he was in the act of putting an arrest in the 'big

---

[2] "Police Reorganized", The Indianapolis News – May 21, 1873, 4, http://indiamond6.ulib.iupui.edu/cdm/compoundobject/collection/IN/id/10679/rec/1

room.' Burley punished several of them severely, while their comrades slunk away from the contest." [3]

August 18, 1873:

A news brief in the Indianapolis News this date stated that the Police Board had dismissed Conrad Burley as assistant turnkey at the City Jail and appointed William Porter.[4]

---

[3] "Minor Mention", The Indianapolis News – July 1, 1873, 3, http://indiamond6.ulib.iupui.edu/cdm/compoundobject/collection/IN/id/5100/rec/1

[4] "The Police Board", The Indianapolis News – August 18, 1873, 3, http://indiamond6.ulib.iupui.edu/cdm/compoundobject/collection/IN/id/5425/rec/11

The Indianapolis Police Force – April 1874[5] Turnkey William M. Porter, African-American, is identified as being in this photograph, 2nd from left.

William M. Porter (1841-1910) was reportedly scratched badly by a strong African-American female prisoner on April 20, 1874. After he was alleged to have allowed the release of a prisoner, he was replaced on May 17, 1874 by John T. Mahorney.

Mahorney was also an African-American and one of the most intellectual men on the force it would turn out. During his interesting life, he authored a biography of Senator Steven Sumner, earned several patents and took his family to London to experience other cultures. Upon returning

[5] IMPD Lichtenberger History Room.

to Indiana, he settled in Irvington, an Indianapolis suburb and enrolled his two children in Butler University. His daughter Gertrude Mahorney became the first African-American in Indiana to earn a college degree, in 1887. She earned her Master's there in 1889.[6] He left the police department in 1876.

On May 12, 1876[7], the police board, which did the hiring and firing for the Metropolitan Police Force, reviewing applications for hire to the police department.   Included on this list (below) were six African-American men.   These were:
Thomas Hart
Benjamin Young
William Christy *
William Whitaker
Philip Franklin
John Minor

* Although William Christy wasn't hired the next day, he lived to see his daughter

---

[6] The Indianapolis News, June 25, 1890.
[7] "Police Appointees", The Indianapolis News – May 12, 1876, 4,
http://indiamond6.ulib.iupui.edu/cdm/compoundobject/collection/IN/id/9739/rec/1

Emma Christy Baker become the first female IPD officer in 1918.

The following day, Saturday, May 13, 1876, five African-Americans were selected to be appointed to the police force: Benjamin Young, William Whitaker, Philip Franklin and Thomas Hart, John Minor and Carter Temple Jr.[8] Carter Temple Jr.'s name is not on the following list due to an apparent omission, but his name is listed in the May 13, 1876 issue of the *News (see below)*.

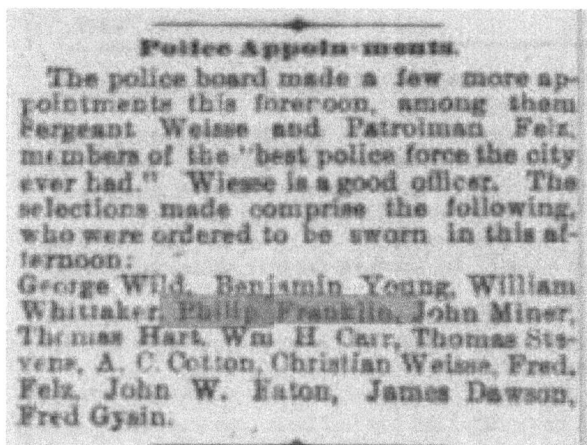

Police Appointments.

The police board made a few more appointments this forenoon, among them Sergeant Weisse and Patrolman Felz, members of the "best police force the city ever had." Wiesse is a good officer. The selections made comprise the following, who were ordered to be sworn in this afternoon:

George Wild, Benjamin Young, William Whittaker, Philip Franklin, John Miner, Thomas Hart, Wm. H. Carr, Thomas Stevens, A. C. Cotton, Christian Weisse, Fred. Felz, John W. Eaton, James Dawson, Fred Gysin.

The Indianapolis News – May 13, 1876

---

[8] "Police Appointments", The Indianapolis News – May 13, 1876, 4,
http://indiamond6.ulib.iupui.edu/cdm/compoundobject/collection/IN/id/9844/rec/1

The Indianapolis News – May 15, 1876

Officer Carter Temple Jr. – ca.1883[9]

---

[9] Cecelia Boler and Reginald Temple.

On May 24, 1876, more appointments were made, including Benjamin Thornton "colored", who would make a name for himself with the Indianapolis Police Department. [10]

Years later, Ben Thornton described the hiring process:

"Twenty-three years ago today I was appointed a member of the police force,

[10] "Police Appointments", The Indianapolis News – May 24, 1876, 4, http://indiamond6.ulib.iupui.edu/cdm/compoundobject/collection/IN/id/9664/rec/1

together with five other colored men and eight white men. Of the six colored men, there are (now) two— Carter Temple and myself. These men were put on the different departments as a trial test, to see how they would compare with the white men. Whether the experiment was a success or a failure, I will leave to the Judgment of the good people of this city. All that I ask is an even break and a fair show, and we shall demonstrate, that we are worthy of all-that we are entrusted with."[11]

Five of the first African-American policemen, specifically Benjamin Young, Walter Whitaker, Carter Temple, Edward Harris and Benjamin Thornton used their resources to assist newly arrived African-American families to purchase a home and getting a job.[12]

In the month of June 1876, Officer William Whitaker attempted to stop two buggies on North Tennessee Street and arrest the

[11]   Benjamin T. Thornton, "An Old Policeman", *The Indianapolis News*, May 25, 1899, 7,
http://indiamond6.ulib.iupui.edu/cdm/compoundobject/collection/IN/id/61519/rec/18
     [12] "Glimpses of the Negro in Indianapolis 1876-1976 by Mrs. Ida Webb Bryant.

occupants in each, for fast driving. One of the men shot Whitaker in the arm and no arrests were made. Whitaker survived.

December 16, 1876: Police Action Shooting

Crum Brown escaped from Marion County Jail by leaping from a second-floor window in late 1876. He was described as a deadly character and a "wanted dead or alive" order was issued. On December 16, 1876, Patrolman Carter Temple came upon Brown and began a lengthy chase, which covered a large part of the northwestern part of the city. Temple traced him to a Mrs. Ross's residence on Lafayette Road, near the White River. As Brown tried to cross the White River, the two men began firing at each other. Brown crossed half way across on the ice, turned and fired at Officer Temple.

Officer Temple fell down to avoid being shot. He struggled to regain his footing on the ice and seeing the wanted man running away, sat up, took careful aim and fired. Officer Carter Temple shot Crum Brown in the back, seriously wounding him. The shooting was ruled justifiable.[13][14] [15]

Officer John Minor was assigned as a Turnkey to the new Sixth Street Station jail on the north side of town. Despite being assigned as the jailor, John was very active outside of the jail, being called out constantly to assist citizens, several of these incidents being detailed later. He did this until his employment ended May 31, 1880.

The city had been divided into districts and from the beginning, African-American men were restricted to specific districts which were predominately African-American. The 1877 police roster[16] shows them being assigned to the 3rd and 11th Districts. This practice would continue into the 1960's.

---

[13] "Recaptured and Shot", The Indianapolis News – December 18, 1876, 1, http://indiamond6.ulib.iupui.edu/cdm/compoundobject/collection/IN/id/9514/rec/2

[15] Unknown Newspaper clipping, dated February 21, 1897.
[16] 1877 Indianapolis City Directory by S.E. Tilford & Co.

On June 19, 1877 at 3 a.m., a burglar cut the screen window shutter of Mr. Myron Dickson of 850 N. Meridian St. and entered the house. Aroused and waiting for him, Dickson fired three shots at the suspect as he chased him through the yard. Officers Benjamin Young and William Whitaker heard the shots and ran to the scene. They saw the suspect lying on the pavement, wounded, on Tinker Street. They conveyed him to Central Station with a wound in the thigh.[17]

After the 1873 political change, the police department became extremely politicized, to the point where if two Democrats were hired, two Republicans had to be hired to keep the balance. This extended to the hiring of African-Americans also. If one was hired who was Republican, an African-American Democrat had to be hired. Just about every year in the 1870-80's, the police force would be reorganized, some new men being appointed, others being dropped.

---

[17] "A Healthy Shot", June 19, 1877: The Indianapolis News, 4, http://indiamond6.ulib.iupui.edu/cdm/compoundobject/collection/IN/id/10549/rec/1

May 27, 1879: The New Police Force

"At the meeting of the police board yesterday, the following new appointments were made: *Samuel Herren* (colored), Ben. F. Johnson, Leonard Crane, Webb Robinson, Melville Havens, Elwood Sands, AL Taffe, Eugene Saulcy and Edward P. Doody, turnkey, Adolphus Shafer, cook, William Franklin, janitor central station, John Widie, Anthony Rogers, John Weber, Andrew Buchanan and Michael Rafferty. The officers dropped are F. M. Harris, *Nathan Ward*, Hiram Altland, *G. W. Hilliard*, Henry Ward, Chris. Wilson, cook, and Oliver Mosby, janitor at the central station.   The force will be sworn in at 6 o'clock tonight when the new beats will be assigned." [18]   (African-Americans placed in italics by author.)

The citizens of Indianapolis were getting adjusted to the idea of African-American

---

[18]   "The New Police Force", The Indianapolis News – May 27, 1879, 4,
http://indiamond6.ulib.iupui.edu/cdm/compoundobject/collection/IN/id/14735/rec/2

police officers, as shown in these two articles in Indianapolis papers:

December 6, 1879:

"A gentleman who was a former resident of this city, but has been out West for four or five years, and has returned for a visit, remarked while passing along Indiana avenue, "that everything was so orderly that it did not seem to be the same old thoroughfare." He was apprised of the fact that the avenue is under the guardianship of three of the most efficient policeman in the city, viz, Thornton, Temple and Hart."[19]

May 8, 1880:

"R.W. Wells, Carter Temple, Ben Thornton, Thomas Hart and Minor are the colored officers on the police force. They are admitted by all to be the very best men on the force-hence they should be retained in the positions they have held with such credit to themselves, their race, and the

---

[19] The Indianapolis Journal – December 6, 1879,
http://indiamond6.ulib.iupui.edu/cdm/compoundobject/collection/IN/id/15249/rec/1

city. Retain these men and give us a few more of the same kind." [20]

The Police Board made changes in the African-American police assignments in June of 1880.[21] They wanted African-American officers Carter Temple, Ben Thornton and Richard Wells to take a new man under their wing and break them in. Beat changes made were:

Ed Harris from the 21st Ward moves to join Carter Temple on his beat.

Ben Thornton moved to the 2nd District, along with Henry Holt of the 1st Ward.

Richard Wells is joined on his old beat by Ephraim Palmer.

Thomas Hart remains on his beat in District 4.

---

[20]   The Indianapolis Leader – May 8, 1880,
http://indiamond6.ulib.iupui.edu/cdm/compoundobject/collect
ion/IN/id/20037/rec/1
[21]   The Indianapolis Leader – June 5, 1880,
http://indiamond6.ulib.iupui.edu/cdm/compoundobject/collect
ion/IN/id/19010/rec/1

On June 1, 1881, the police board named the following assignments for African-Americans on the police department:[22]

Day Men
Fourth District – Thomas Hart

Night Men
Second District – Ed Harris
Third District – Henry Holt
Fourth District- Carter Temple, Benj. Thornton

On Saturday, October 1, 1881, Patrolman Henry Holt (African-American), attempted to arrest George Fry, a "hoodlum". Fry cut him with a razor, causing serious injuries. Fry escaped. He was apprehended in Martinsville, Indiana by the Morgan County Sheriff. He was returned to Indianapolis on October 6th. [23] [24]

---

[22] "The Police Assignments", The Indianapolis News – June 2, 1881, 3,
http://indiamond6.ulib.iupui.edu/cdm/compoundobject/collection/IN/id/16521/rec/2
[23] "City News", The Indianapolis News, October 3, 1881, 3,
http://indiamond6.ulib.iupui.edu/cdm/compoundobject/collection/IN/id/17441/rec/1
[24] "City News", The Indianapolis News – October 7, 1881, 4,
http://indiamond6.ulib.iupui.edu/cdm/compoundobject/collection/IN/id/17356/rec/5

The following story illustrates how heavily one's political beliefs could affect their career with the Indianapolis Police force.

The Indianapolis News – September 12, 1882

Patrolman Henry Holt was suspended from duty for 30 days. There were no charges filed against him but the News suggested it had something to do with a Dr. Elbert being a candidate for the state legislature. Holt was described as "one of the most vigilant and efficient" men on the force. He was held in high regard by Chief Robert Williamson.[25]

On April 14, 1883, the Police Board that had existed for years was replaced by the Board of Public Safety. This board consisted of aldermen who appointed new police officers, dismissed others and administered disciplinary action. This came about from a legislative act that required an equal number of Democrats and

[25] "Suspended from Duty", The Indianapolis News – September 12, 1882, 4,
http://indiamond6.ulib.iupui.edu/cdm/compoundobject/collection/IN/id/19145/rec/1

Republicans among the police officers. For some time, the Mayor of Indianapolis had controlled the appointments to the force.

There are five African-Americans depicted in this photograph[26] taken in May 1890 of the entire Indianapolis Police force.

---

[26] IMPD Lichtenberger History Room.

INDIANAPOLIS COLORED POLICE.

March 1889 African-American Indianapolis Police Officers[27]

27   The Freeman – March 16, 1889, from Facebook site Zeke Town, accessed May 13, 2014.
https://www.facebook.com/ZekeTown?filter=1

"The Yellow Bridge" [28]

The "Old Yellow Bridge", over the canal at Indiana Avenue, was once a police deadline between the African-American residents north of the canal and the "Bungaloos", who attacked them and who met at Military Park to the south.

Research shows the Bungaloos fighting other gangs, White and Black, as early as 1897. Pitched battles between the Bungaloos and African-Americans trying to

---

[28] IMPD Lichtenberger History Room.

enjoy themselves occurred in the western part of downtown on a regular basis.

One of the worst incidents involving the "Bungaloos", described as young white hooligans, occurred on Sunday, July 21, 1901 at Fairview Park. An estimated 10,000 people were at the park when a riot broke out between the Bungaloos and some African-American boys.

The Bungaloos chased them into a pavilion, where police in the park protected them. "The Bungaloos" stoned the crowd and fired several shots. After failing to get ahold of the Governor by phone to call in the militia, the police in the park called for 15 additional officers, who did arrive.

A bystander was shot in the neck, two men were badly beaten with clubs and scores of men and women were stoned. This was described as an old feud between the Bungaloos and African-Americans on the west side of town.[29]

---

[29] "Riot in Indianapolis", The Clinton (Iowa) Mirror, July 27, 1901, 2,
http://news.google.com/newspapers?nid=2281&dat=19010727&id=OncoAAAAIBAJ&sjid=BAYGAAAAIBAJ&pg=4044,390928

A second "riot" occurred at the same place on Sunday, August 26, 1901. In this similar incident, dozens of terrified African-Americans ran toward police headquarters for safety, closely pursued by the Bungaloos, who managed to catch and beat some before IPD officers could reach them. Police to their credit charged into the Bungaloos and arrested several of the ringleaders.

The Neighborhoods they patrolled

There were two distinct neighborhoods populated by African-Americans in 19th century Indianapolis.[30] The oldest was known as "Pat Ward's Bottoms" and was located on the northwest side of town, along the canal, on W. 11th Street. It was established during and after the Civil War. It was part of the 34th District. The second was farther north of that area, along what is now known as Dr. Martin Luther King Jr. Street. This area seems to correspond with

---

[30] Richard B. Pierce, Polite Protest: The Political Economy of Race in Indianapolis, 1920-1970, 11.
http://books.google.com/books?id=H3-z55__320C&pg=PA11&dq=pat+ward's+bottoms+indianapolis&hl=en&sa=X&ei=viZFU4j2Fsa9yAHGs4GICw&ved=0CDkQ6AEwAQ#v=onepage&q=pat%20ward's%20bottoms%20indianapolis&f=false

what 40-year IPD veteran "Jack" Hadley described as "old District 35", an area between 9th and 16th Streets and West Street and Capitol Avenue. This was his first assignment in 1920.[31]

Patrolman Jack Hadley

[31] "Sgt. Hadley In Local Police Dept. 25 Years", *Indianapolis Recorder* – September 15, 1945, 1, http://indiamond6.ulib.iupui.edu/cdm/compoundobject/collection/IRecorder/id/26491/rec/1

Years later, a third neighborhood where African-Americans were allowed to live was located on the east side, near Douglas Park. This area is now known as Brightwood.[32] Jack Hadley called this the "badlands."

In July 1948, a "slum" clearance program began by the Indianapolis Redevelopment Commission targeted Pat Ward's Bottoms. Their target neighborhood roughly embraced the area from Tenth Street to Sixteenth and from West Street on the East to Fall Creek on the West. It was described at that time as one of the worst areas in Indianapolis, crime ridden and extremely neglected. The homes were around 75 years old and many still had outside toilets. This area comprised Attucks H.S.

32 Ibid, p.58

August 25, 1886

First African-American Joins the IPD Detective Squad

Detective Benjamin Thornton[33]

---

[33] IMPD Lichtenberger History Room.

On August 25, 1886[34], Officer Benjamin Thornton, who had been patrolling the streets with Carter Temple since 1878, was promoted to detective. Thornton described how it happened in an 1896 newspaper interview:

On the evening of August 20, 1886, Superintendent of Police Michael O'Donnell ordered Ben to come to his office after roll call. As he recalled in 1896, Ben said, "I had no idea of what was in store for me and I supposed that I was to be 'called down', for something I had done. O'Donnell was brusque in manner and always gave his commands in a short, abrupt way. I was considerably relieved when he informed me that he could use me to greater advantage in citizens' clothes, and directed me to report for duty without my uniform the next morning." IPD official history gives the date that Benjamin Thornton became a detective as August 25, 1886.

This was the first time an African-American held the rank of Detective with this

---

[34]   IPD History,
http://www.indy.gov/eGov/City/DPS/IMPD/About/History/Pages/IPDHistory.aspx

department. He was very familiar with the criminals in Indianapolis and their activities, which greatly aided him in solving cases.

Det. Thornton solved several murders, including the slaying of Willie Roberts in a saloon. Through his investigation, John Coleman was arrested in St. Louis, Missouri for the murder and Thornton left to pick him up on October 15, 1890. "In our business, the least little thing sometimes leads to the greatest results", Thornton frequently said.

Typical of Det. Thornton's activities was this 1886 article from a Fort Wayne, Indiana newspaper:

"Officer Ben Thornton, of the Indianapolis metropolitan police, was in the city yesterday after a horse thief, who was located here. Thornton is a colored man, but a very "fly" cop in his line of business. He says that in the past year fifty horses have been stolen at Indian, spoils, and not one of them recovered. Sheriff Nelson records but the loss of one horse in the past year in

Allen County, and gave that thief a big chase for two days."[35]

Det. Thornton went all over the United States to pick up suspects and gained a national reputation as an excellent detective by the time of his death, June 18, 1900.   His death was potentially in the line of duty as he contracted pneumonia while staking out the residence in a driving rain, of Edward Ruthven. Ruthven had murdered a Cleveland policeman that summer.   Although there was talk of replacing Thornton on the detective squad with another African-American, that did not occur and there is no evidence an African-American served there until 1919.

[35] The Fort Wayne Indiana Sentinel – November 11, 1886, 4, http://www.newspapers.com/newspage/29110896/

Detective Benjamin Thornton –
Departmental Photograph[36]

April 12, 1895:

An embarrassing situation arose where a
man named Alex Tyler was dismissed from
the force after it was discovered he was not
a White man, as first supposed. He had
been appointed to fill a position for a White
officer. When his true race was discovered,
he was terminated because there were then
no openings for an African-American.

---

[36] IMPD Lichtenberger History Room.

"A delegation of about fifteen colored men, headed by Councilman Puryear, was before the Board of Public Safety, protesting against the refusal to put Alex Tyler on the police force, after his appointment as patrolman had been announced. The delegation insisted that men should be appointed for merit, regardless of color. Afterward the board determined to Increase the number of colored men on the force to ten. At present, there are eight. N. E. Clarke and Lafayette Kennedy were appointed; both are colored."[37]

October 29, 1895: 29 IPD Officers Dismissed
The Board of Public Safety met at 5:30 p.m. this date, to finalize a list of officers who would be dismissed. Although some were charged with some kind of offense, this was likely another politically related purge which was an almost annual event in the 19th century. Several African-American

---

[37] "Colored and White Policemen", The Indianapolis News – April 12, 1895, 2,
http://indiamond6.ulib.iupui.edu/cdm/compoundobject/collection/IN/id/46493/rec/1

officers were dismissed, by letter, effective November 1st: [38]

William Wheeler

William Wheeler – Republican (he would be rehired and serve until 1927)

Lafayette Kennedy – Republican

William Winn

---

[38]   The Indianapolis News – October 29, 1895,
http://indiamond6.ulib.iupui.edu/cdm/compoundobject/collect
ion/IN/id/49086/rec/1

The new Indianapolis Police Department headquarters building, opened on March 9, 1898, stood at 35 S. Alabama Street. It was razed in 1962.[39]

On December 15, 1899, the Board of Public Safety dismissed almost a dozen police officers for various reasons (Including African-American Officer Earl E. Titus). The police officers protested this through an attorney and sued for back pay of $153 per officer. Although most were not rehired, on February 11, 1901 a legislative act set up a system of merit grading system. There were four grades for Patrolmen, which were

---

[39]   IMPD Lichtenberger History Room.

based on longevity.   For another 74 years however, the promotional system at IPD was controlled by politics and handled unevenly at best.   For the African-American officer, promotion was not something he could expect.

On March 1, 1901, four African-American men went on duty with the police department, Benjamin W. Tanzy, John W. Cousins, John T. Ball and Louis W. Montgomery.[40]   This was the largest number hired at once since 1876.   This brought the total number of African-Americans on the police department to 12.

---

[40] "Twelve New Policemen", The Indianapolis News, February 21, 1901, 12,
http://indiamond6.ulib.iupui.edu/cdm/compoundobject/collection/IN/id/67801/rec/1

March 1901:

12 African-Americans now Working for IPD
Indianapolis Police Department Roster:
African-Americans – 1901 [41]

James Admire

Simpson Hart [42]

Patrolmen: (total of 12)
James Admire
John T. Bell
John W. Cousins
James Crabtree
Simpson Hart
Edward Harris
Ben Lee

---

[41] The *Indianapolis Recorder* December 21, 1901, 2,
http://indiamond6.ulib.iupui.edu/cdm/compoundobject/collect
ion/IRecorder/id/3643/rec/3
    [42] Photos from IMPD Lichtenberger History Room.

L. W. Montgomery
B. W. Tansy
William Winn
Gab Jones
G.H. Goens

February 1913

"Guardian of the Chute"

Charles Carter[43]

---

[43] IMPD Lichtenberger History Room.

A story in the Indianapolis Star on February 23, 1913 described what was probably agreed to be the worst part of town. This was a primitive area was known as Wild Cat Chute and lay between West 13th and 14th Streets, a little way west of Indiana Avenue. No one except the residents of that area and the police ever visited there, the police advising that nobody venture into that area if they feared for their safety.

"The Chute" was a narrow court surrounded by run down tenements, which shared a common backyard where fights were common. Police were showered with bricks when they tried to make an arrest. "Dope fiends", drunks and women of low character frequented "The Chute." The nickname came from a woman who, when officers tried to arrest her, fought so ferociously, she tore an officer's uniform to shreds. After finally getting her under control, the officer remarked that she was a "tough customer". She replied with a hiss, "Indeed, I'm not a woman, I'm a wild cat", sinking her teeth into his arm to prove the point.

In this area, Officer Charles Carter was assigned a regular beat. By 1913, Officer Carter had been on this beat for several years and he declared that most of the bad characters had died or moved to other parts. The Star declared him "Guardian of the Chute."[44]

African-American "nightmen" in 1916.
Left to right: John Mosbey, John Coleman, Thomas Hopson.

---

[44] "Wild Cat Chute in Death Stand", The Indianapolis Sunday Star, February 23, 1913, 7, Ancestry.com. The *The Indianapolis Star* (Indianapolis, Indiana) [database on-line]. Provo, UT, USA: Ancestry.com Operations Inc, 2006.

June 15, 1918

The Indianapolis Police Department hires its first African-American Female Officers

Emma Baker

Mary Mays

On June 15, 1918, 14 women were appointed to the Indianapolis Police Department. Among these first policewomen were two African-American women, Emma (Christy) Baker and Mary (Roberts) Mays.

The first 13 women hired as police officers for IPD were in their 40-50's and selected due to their previous employment backgrounds, which were nurses, matrons or people who worked with juveniles. Emma (Christy) Baker), age 49, was selected in part because she was a well-known figure in the African-American community, helping to run her father William Christy's laundry. Mary Mays spent over 20-years as a visiting nurse for the Indianapolis Flower Mission, ministering to thousands of the city's poor.

The women were issued badges and were paid $3.25 a day, the same as a male officer. However, they did not wear uniforms. They would do plain clothes detective work in local stores, looking for shoplifters from 1918-1922. Their primary duties revolved around protecting the female youth of Indianapolis from being corrupted morally. This included being dance matrons, going into arcades and bars, making sure no underage females were there.

By and large, the women officers were praised for the job they did and Officer Emma Baker in particular, came in for praise by the *Indianapolis Recorder* throughout her career. Even after being shifted to the Juvenile Aid Division in 1922, she worked hard in the probation department. She was the only African-American there in 1931. When Emma Baker retired in March of 1939, she was the only African-American policewoman at IPD.

George "Slim" Brown

Inducted into the U.S. Army August 22, 1918 and served in the 109th Pioneer Infantry. He was honorably discharged July 23, 1919. Served IPD 1922-1935.

May 28, 1919

Three African-Americans Promoted to the rank of Sergeant

Top: Joshua Spearis Bottom, L-R: George Sneed, Edward Trabue

"First Colored Sergeants"

"Sneed and Trabue are both colored, and it is said to be the first time in the history of the department that two colored men have been given the rank of sergeant in the detective department.   Both men have made excellent records."

On this same date, 36-year veteran African-American Joshua Spearis was promoted from Patrolman to Sergeant in the Emergency Squad. [45]

---

[45]   *The Indianapolis Star* – May 28, 1919, 13,
http://www.newspapers.com/newspage/6887854/

Officer John M. Newby, age 43, a 9-year veteran African-American officer, suffered an apparent heart attack while fishing in Fall Creek near 20th Street. He slipped down the bank into Fall Creek and drowned. [47]

---

[46] IMPD Lichtenberger History Room.
[47]   The Indianapolis News - June 29, 1919, 5,
http://www.newspapers.com/newspage/6893665/

March 3, 1920

Gun battle with Henry "Hellcat" Thomas

48

One of the most famed local desperadoes in Indianapolis in 1920 was Henry "Hellcat" Thomas. A thief, he envisioned himself as a western outlaw after reading numerous

---

48 IMPD Historic Photograph Archives

dime novels and detective magazines, including wearing western garb. He strutted up and down Indiana Avenue wearing his cowboy outfit and distributed post cards of him wearing it. He was described by IPD Detective Sergeant Claude White as a fairly nice person until he was provoked. His life took a very violent turn after the death of his two children in a house fire in the spring of 1920.

After the fire, Hellcat and his wife moved into a home at 1336 N. West Street. Two detectives, George Sneed and Edward Trabue, both African-Americans, had been looking for Hellcat in connection to stolen goods. They raided his home on February 21, 1920. They recovered $4,000 in merchandise and arrested his wife. While the detectives were in the home, Hellcat was outside and watched through the window.   He related to his acquaintances that he refrained from shooting them due to the proximity of his wife.

The arrest of his wife made Henry Thomas angry and he wrote a threatening letter to Detective Sneed as related in the 2006

History of the Indianapolis Police Department:

"I thought I'd drop you a few lines to give you fair warning about that goods you took from our house at 1336 N. West Street. You and your partner blame it on the woman but that's a damn lie and you all know it. That woman didn't know anything about it. I am the man-I did it myself. I will give you until the second of March to take that woman out of jail. If she ain't out then, I am going to kill you and Trabue too."

Hellcat wrote a second note, directed at Sneed and Trabue which read: *"I am direct from Hell…I'll let all the women live, but I'll kill all the men…I live 300 miles south of Hell, I am the original Hellcat and I shoot to kill."*

Undaunted by death threats, Detectives Sneed and Trabue went through the neighborhood Hellcat lived in, running down rumors of his whereabouts. They thought they had him when they had a report he was at 17th and Boulevard Place. IPD sent numerous officers that time, but Henry Thomas was not there upon arrival.

George Sneed wore his WWI uniform on March 3, 1920 when he started a block by block search of the near west side in search of Hellcat, as a disguise. While walking near an alley at 12th and West Streets, they saw man eating doughnuts in the alley in a light rain. It was Henry "Hellcat" Thomas. He was wearing a raincoat instead of his usual cowboy outfit.

Unfortunately, Detective Sneed didn't realize it was Hellcat at first. He thought he was acting suspiciously however, so he grabbed Hellcat's wrist. Hellcat threw his arms up to shield his face, crying "Please mister, don't shoot me."

Sneed, taken back by the sniveling man in front of him, relaxed his grip for a second. That was all the time Hellcat needed to jerk loose, run a few steps, pull out a pistol and begin firing at Sneed. They were about 20 paces apart. Sneed fell to the ground, army training perhaps and returned fire with his own automatic, but missed.

Hellcat missed all of his shots as well, apparently not being an expert marksman. The story George Sneed told later was that

Hellcat approached him at this point and at point blank range, pulled the trigger with the gun pointing at the detective. The gun failed to fire, sparing Sneed's life. Hellcat then hid behind a vegetable cart and then a telephone pole as George Sneed called to him, "You'd better give up. You are out of cartridges." Hellcat shook his head from side to side and took off down the alley.

At this time, Detective Edward Trabue arrived and started firing at Hellcat as he ran. Hellcat hid in a shed in the rear of 536 W. 12th Street. Someone called this in on the Gamewell communications system and IPD responded in force. Sergeant Maurice Murphy and his driver Patrolman Harry McGlenn, having finished a run, pulled up in front of IPD Headquarters. Desk Captain Albert Ray called out a window of the building to them, directing them to go to the scene of the shooting. They were joined by Lieutenant Edward C. Ball and Lieutenant Herbert R. Fletcher in Murphy's car.

As these and other officers began pouring into the near west side, Murphy's squad of officers; approached the shed where Hellcat was in fact hiding.   Sergeant Murphy and Lieutenant Ball started walking toward the shed. Hellcat made a break for it.   Lt. Ball yelled "There he is!" and fired three times before his pistol jammed. Hellcat fired two shots at the same time.

Sergeant Murphy was standing behind Ball and he was hit, falling on his back in the mud.   Murphy was carried through the yard and put in the police car and rushed to city hospital. Doctors said bullets had penetrated his abdomen and left hand. Back at the shooting scene, Lieutenant Herbert Fletcher heard the shooting and closed on Hellcat's position. A witness directed him to where he was hiding.

Entering an alley, Fletcher came up behind Hellcat, who was crouching behind a box, reloading his weapon.   Lieutenant Fletcher unloaded with his weapon. His first shot hit Hellcat in the throat, but the suspect still got up and fled south across 12th Street through yards to Darnell Street, a small street between 11th and 12th Streets.   He ended up in the back of 629 W. 11th Street. Sitting down on the ground, attempting to reload his .45 Colt automatic, he keeled over dead at the age of 35.

IPD Sergeant Maurice Murphy was 42 years old, a native of Ireland. He had joined the department April 3, 1907 and had a wife and 7-year old daughter Mary. As he died in the hospital, his last words were "Take care of my Mary."

In the aftermath of this, one of the most dramatic gun battles in IPD history, Detective George Sneed and Detective Edward Trabue were decorated for bravery. During their running gun battle with Hellcat, they continued to advance under fire, showing incredible bravery. [49]

---

[49]   2006 History of IPD – pp.37-39

January 2, 1922

Two Policewomen Appointed to IPD

Hettie Brewer   Mamie Shelton

When the new city administration took office, January 2, 1922, two new African-American policewomen were appointed to the Indianapolis Police Department. Hettie Brewer formerly owned a restaurant on Indiana Avenue and was involved in women's clubs. Mamie Shelton was a widow. Leaving IPD at the same time was Mary Mays, giving the department three women of color. Mamie died of a stroke nine months after being appointed, hours after going home from her beat.

June 18, 1922

Officer William Whitfield Shot in the Line of Duty

50

Officer William Whitfield, 37, was shot by an unknown gunman on Sunday, June 18, 1922, in an alley just west of 3600 North College Avenue shortly after 11:00 pm. Officer Whitfield was taken to City hospital where he lingered near death for several months. He died on November 27,

---

50   IPD History in Memorium, accessed May 15, 2014, http://www.indy.gov/eGov/City/DPS/IMPD/About/Memoriam/Pages/wwhitfield.aspx

1922. Officer Whitfield was the first African-American IPD officer to give his life in the line of duty. His death was not given the usual rigorous investigation that other line of duty deaths have been given.

There is a question about why he was assigned alone to a "white" beat on the night of his shooting, which had never been done. His grave lay unmarked until the research of IPD Officer Wayne Sharp, in 1998 departmental personnel led a collection effort that resulted in a headstone being placed on his grave in Crown Hill Cemetery. [51] [52]

[51] IPD History In Memorium, accessed April 9, 2014, http://www.indy.gov/eGov/City/DPS/IMPD/About/Memoriam/Pages/wwhitfield.aspx
[52] Wayne Sharp, Legends in Blue, 2002, 66-67

In 2013, the Indianapolis Metropolitan Police Department instituted a program of placing memorial signs at each location where a former law enforcement officer was killed in the line of duty, The Fallen Officer's Legacy Project, which was the brainchild of Ben Staletovich. The program started May 13, 2013 with a ceremony at McCord Park. One of the very first memorial placards to be placed was to remember Officer William Whitfield.
Above, Sergeant Steve Staletovich places it.

December 1922

DETECTIVE CLAUDE WHITE

Officer Claude White survives desperate fight

In mid-December 1922, Officer Claude White was Involved in an incident in which he himself was shot and badly wounded and then returned fire, killing his assailant. Near Senate and 11th Avenue, a shot rang out from a saloon. Officer White, who was off duty, charged through the saloon door as a 2nd shot was fired, which struck him in the right arm. White returned fire until his assailant fell to the floor.

Then from behind, the dead man's brother attacked White with a knife. He slashed at White's throat repeatedly but White was saved by a scarf he had put on that morning due to the cold weather. White's gun was almost empty but he managed to get a shot off which struck the man as he ran from the scene. The suspect managed to get back up and run, being chased by Officer White for several blocks. White stopped the chase and returned to the saloon due to heavy loss of blood. [53]

January 16, 1923

First four African-Americans Assigned to the IPD Traffic Division

On January 16, 1923, another groundbreaking move was made by assigning four African-Americans to the IPD Traffic Division, which was considered a promotion.[54] These men were: (Clockwise

[53] Opal Tandy, "The Human Side of the Law", *Indianapolis Recorder* - January 8, 1938, 2,
http://indiamond6.ulib.iupui.edu/cdm/compoundobject/collection/IRecorder/id/60319/rec/1
[54] "In Shakeup", *Indianapolis Recorder* – August 22, 1931, 1, (mentions date Roy S. Kennedy assigned to Traffic as Jan 16, 1923),

from top left) Officer John F. Buchanan,
Officer Roy S. Kennedy, Officer John
Coleman, Officer Claude C. White.

Taken between December October 1923 &
June 1924. All of IPD's African-American
officers posed for this picture on the steps of
City Hall.

1925

George Sneed becomes first African-American Lieutenant on IPD

55

George Sneed had served six years as a Detective Sergeant for IPD, when in 1925 he was promoted to the rank of Acting Lieutenant, a first for an African-American

---

55 IMPD Lichtenberger History Room.

with this department. [56] He served in the
Uniform Division according to the
Indianapolis Recorder of May 31, 1947.[57]
In 1926 he was reduced back to Sergeant.
He held this rank until May 28, 1947 when
he was again made a field Lieutenant,
replacing Preston Heater. George Sneed
was known as the "father of negro
policemen" and also as one of the finest
officers who ever worked for the
Indianapolis Police Department.

---

[56] *Indianapolis Recorder* – January 23, 1926, 1,
http://indiamond6.ulib.iupui.edu/cdm/compoundobject/collect
ion/IRecorder/id/37480/rec/1
[57] "Det. Geo. Sneed Named Lieut.: Heater Retires", *Indianapolis
Recorder* – May 31, 1947, 1,
http://indiamond6.ulib.iupui.edu/cdm/compoundobject/collection/IR
ecorder/id/90866/rec/1

July 9, 1926

Officer John F. Buchanan Killed in the Line of Duty

[58]

On July 9, 1926, a man named Gene Alger tried to steal a man's car. Alger was taken to Patrolman John Mosby. As Mosby and his partner, Patrolman Jesse Hadley called police headquarters from 201 N. Capitol Avenue, Alger jumped up and fled the scene. He pulled a .45 pistol and from a doorway, fired at Mosby and Hadley (both African-Americans). They returned his fire.

---

[58] IPD History: In Memorium,
http://www.indy.gov/eGov/City/DPS/IMPD/About/Memoriam/
Pages/jbuchanan.aspx

Continuing to fire as he ran between the Plaza hotel and the Beyer hotel at 225 N. Capitol Avenue, he broke a window at the Beyer, climbing in, where he took the owner, Mr. E.A. Beyer hostage. From his post at Capitol and Indiana Avenues, Patrolman John F. Buchanan heard the firing and was directed by a witness to the second floor of the Beyer hotel where Alger was hiding in a closet with a hostage.

Buchanan called for Alger to come out. Alger fired twice, striking Officer Buchanan above the heart with one of them.

Alger ran past the prone body of Officer Buchanan, left the hotel, shot a bystander and pistol whipped another. He hijacked a car and forced the driver to leave the scene. Alger was shot and wounded by Officer Carl Sheets at New York and Illinois Streets. He and the civilians he injured survived. Officer John Buchanan died instantly.

Buchanan had made history on January 16, 1923 when he and three other African-American officers became the first to be assigned to the IPD Traffic Division. Chief of Police Claude F. Johnson said "He was popular and efficient and in his death the Indianapolis Police Department loses a good man." [59] [60] [61]

Officer Irving Hardy. He died while serving of illness, 1933.

---

[59]   The original research of IMPD Civilian Jean Ritsema and IPD Detective Wayne Sharp.

[60]   Indianapolis Metropolitan Police Department webpage, accessed April 9, 2014,
http://www.indy.gov/eGov/City/DPS/IMPD/About/Memoriam/Pages/jbuchanan.aspx

[61]   "Gunman Runs Amock: Kills Policeman", *Indianapolis Recorder* – July 17, 1926, 1,
http://indiamond6.ulib.iupui.edu/cdm/compoundobject/collection/IRecorder/id/37687/rec/1

March 9, 1929

Officer Norvel Bennett Commended for Capturing Burglar

62

Norvel Bennett

While patrolling his beat, Officer Norvel Bennett flashed his light into the Kroger grocery at 2134 N. Illinois Street. He saw a man run to the back door of the store. Bennett quickly called the Emergency Squad and Sergeant Hodges and Officer Purcell responded. They found George Andrews still in the store. He was arrested

---

62 IMPD Lichetenberger History Room.

for burglary.   Chief Worley said "I wish to commend Patrolman Norvel Bennett, for his splendid capture of this burglar. If all officers were as faithful in the performance of their duty, as this officer, burglars and other law violators would give this city a wide berth." [63]

November 1, 1930

Detectives Nab 3, Burglaries Cease

With the arrest of Jessie Pope, 20 and James Stewart, 23 by Detectives George Sneed and Claude White, these arrests cleared up 10 robberies. Following these arrests, Sneed and White apprehended John Coleman, 59, who was in possession of stolen goods fenced by the suspects.[64]

---

[63]   "Chief Worley Commends Officer Norvel Bennett", *Indianapolis Recorder* – March 9, 1929, 1, http://indiamond6.ulib.iupui.edu/cdm/compoundobject/collection/IRecorder/id/53967/rec/1

[64]   "Detectives Nab 3, Burglaries Cease", *Indianapolis Recorder* – November 1, 1930, 1, http://indiamond6.ulib.iupui.edu/cdm/compoundobject/collection/IRecorder/id/15438/rec/1

January 3, 1931

Detectives Swoop Down on Thieves

Detective Thomas Hopson[65]

IPD Detectives George Sneed, Claude White, Thomas Hopson and Plez Jones (all African-American), arrested eight suspects at 810 Drake Street, all of whom were heavily armed. After several hours of questioning, the men admitted several street car and grocery store robberies. They were charged with Robbery. [66]

---

[65] IMPD Lichtenberger History Room.

[66] "Detectives Swoop Down on Thieves", *Indianapolis Recorder* – January 3, 1931, 2,

The Edward Pierson Murder Case

Edward Pierson   George Washington

This case, in which IPD Detectives George Sneed and Claude White figured heavily, began in April of 1930 with the murder of Edward D. Pierson, a Chicago auditor of the National Baptist Publishing Board in Scottsburg, Indiana. This murder created a national sensation at the time.

A man identifying himself as George Moorehead had appeared at the home of Pierson in Chicago and arranged to meet Pierson in Louisville, Kentucky. Pierson was last seen alive in Louisville. Pierson was found murdered on the bank of the Muscatatuck River, near Austin, Indiana, April 16, 1930. (37 miles from Louisville). He had been shot 5 times and thrown over a bridge into the river. George Moorehead was an alias used by George Washington, a 41 year old African-American with a criminal history. He was also later suspected of shooting up a court house in Fort Wayne, Indiana.

On June 18, 1930, after shadowing the primary suspect in the Pierson murder case in Indianapolis for several weeks, Detectives George Sneed and Claude White of IPD sat down in the Senate Avenue branch of the Y.M.C.A. They motioned for George Washington over to where they were seated for a little chat. As he sat down, they pulled the chair out from under him and fell upon him, putting handcuffs on. He was armed with a fully loaded revolver. They hadn't planned on arresting him until other suspects were arrested but he appeared ready to leave town so they made their move. The detectives had worked daily on the Pierson murder case for weeks. Washington was indicated by a Scott County, Indiana Grand Jury and held in jail in Scottsburg, Indiana.

On June 25, 1931, the man arrested in the nationally famous Edward Pierson murder case, George Washington, was exonerated by a grand jury. His arrest by George Sneed and Claude White ignited a furor because he was a highly placed figure in the Baptist community. Mr. Pierson was likewise a respected auditor from Chicago.[67] A possible motive in the case was that Pierson had discovered a shortage of $62,000 in the Baptist accounts. During a 1938 interview[68], Claude White recalled working day and night for two months before making an arrest. Although the man was exonerated, White felt that if they had been

---

[67] "Famous Washington-Pierson Case Dismissed", *Indianapolis Recorder* – June 27, 1931, 1, http://indiamond6.ulib.iupui.edu/cdm/compoundobject/collection/IRecorder/id/15429/rec/1

[68] Opal Tandy, "The Human Side of the Law", *Indianapolis Recorder* - January 8, 1938, 2, http://indiamond6.ulib.iupui.edu/cdm/compoundobject/collection/IRecorder/id/60319/rec/1

given more time, they could have solved the case, which remained unsolved.

July 27, 1931:

Alleged Police Slayer Caught in South Returned to City
Richard Perkins, alias Cole, suspected as the killer of IPD Detective Carl W. Heckman on January 3, 1931 before he held up a laundry, truck, was brought to Indianapolis from Chattanooga, Tennessee, by Detectives George Sneed and Claude White. Perkins had been the subject of an intense manhunt. Sneed and White, had followed Perkins' movements since he escaped from Indianapolis. Perkins had been captured at Atlanta, Georgia by an African-American officer there. He was charged with murder.[69] He was electrocuted October 1, 1934.[70]

---

[69] "Alleged Police Slayer Caught in South Returned to City", *Indianapolis Recorder* – August 1, 1931, 1, http://indiamond6.ulib.iupui.edu/cdm/compoundobject/collection/IRecorder/id/15890/rec/1

[70] IPD History: In Memorium, http://www.indy.gov/eGov/City/DPS/IMPD/About/Memoriam/Pages/checkman.aspx

August 1931:

Detective Sergeant Roy Kennedy[71]

In a shakeup at IPD, Detective Sergeant Preston Heater was reduced in rank to 2nd grade patrolman. An 11-year veteran, he had been appointed Detective Sergeant in 1928. Replacing him as Detective Sergeant was Roy S. Kennedy, hired in 1919.[72]

---

[71] IMPD Lichtenberger History Room.

[72] "In Shakeup", *Indianapolis Recorder* – August 22, 1931, 1, http://indiamond6.ulib.iupui.edu/cdm/compoundobject/collection/IRecorder/id/15944/rec/1

September 14, 1931:

Five convicted robbers drew a total of 75 years this date in Criminal Court. They had been convicted of the July 21st holdup of the Walker Theatre, which netted $128. They tied up half a dozen employees in the basement during the robbery. Officers who figured in solving the crime and arrests were: Detectives George Sneed, Claude White, Charles Carter, Preston Heater, Barnaby and Vanzette.[73]

February 2, 1935:

A pharmacy at 502 Indiana Avenue was held up by two men about midnight on Tuesday. They forced him at the point of a gun to hand over merchandise and $32 in cash. A third man stood outside as lookout. This case was assigned to Detective Sergeants George Sneed and John Glenn. Within a few hours they had the suspects in custody. [74]

---

[73] "Walker Theatre Holdup Gang Sentenced to 75 Years", *Indianapolis Recorder* – September 19, 1931, 1, http://indiamond6.ulib.iupui.edu/cdm/compoundobject/collection/IRecorder/id/15980/rec/1

[74] "3 Questioned in Drug Store Robbery", *Indianapolis Recorder* - February 2, 1935, 1,

January 25, 1936

The McCrimmon Case

Ferdinand Holt   Plez Jones[75]

This case, like the case of Henry "Hellcat" Thomas, involved death threats made against Detective Sergeant George Sneed. It stretched over 16 years. It started with the arrest of George McCrimmon, age 23, late in 1935 at 706 Indiana Avenue by Detective Sergeants Ferdinand Holt and Plez Jones.

---

http://indiamond6.ulib.iupui.edu/cdm/compoundobject/collection/IRecorder/id/16974/rec/1
[75] IMPD Lichtenberger History Room.

He was taken by surprise before he could grab a revolver lying nearby. After his arrest, he told Holt of his intention to kill him and Sneed. As far as Plez Jones was concerned, McCrimmon said he was a fine fellow adding he had no intention of ever harming him. "That's the first time any man I have hunted so intently has ever seen it that way", Detective Jones laughingly remarked later.

George McCrimmon, 23, was then held in the Marion County Jail for numerous robberies, burglaries and hold-ups. He made repeated death threats to kill Sneed and Detective Sergeant Ferdinand Holt, who were responsible for arresting McCrimmon's partners.

On January 19, 1936, McCrimmon pulled an old trick on a deputy sheriff, impersonating another prisoner who was being released. He walked out of the jail. McCrimmon's partners. James and Jesse Curry, who boasted they would never be taken alive were later arrested after McCrimmon had been nabbed. Detective Sergeants John Glenn. Sneed, Claude White and Thomas Hopson affected the capture of Jesse Curry, also a paroled convict by a daring dash upon a taxi cab in which Jesse was riding. Though Curry was heavily armed, Detective White entered the cab as it stopped for a traffic signal, and overpowered the gunman before he had time to resist.[76]

Ten days after escaping, on January 29, 1936, George McCrimmon was recaptured. He appeared in February 1936 in Criminal Court, where Judge Frank P. Baker sentenced him to 10-25 years in the state reformatory. Jesse Curry received an identical sentence, while his younger brother James Curry, a minor, received a sentence of 1-10 years. Referring to the death threats against IPD detectives, "Criminal court officials believe that after he has killed so much time, he will change his mind."[77]

Note: This case is continued in 1952.

---

[76] "Offers Reward for Capture of Escaped Bandit", *Indianapolis Recorder* - January 25, 1936 , 1, http://indiamond6.ulib.iupui.edu/cdm/compoundobject/collection/IRecorder/id/22152/rec/1

[77] "Sentenced", *Indianapolis Recorder* - February 8, 1936, 4, http://indiamond6.ulib.iupui.edu/cdm/compoundobject/collection/IRecorder/id/22169/rec/1

October 10, 1936:

David Thompson was stabbed to death after a barroom fight at the Owl Café, 559 Indiana Avenue on September 18, 1936, which was witnessed by numerous persons. After a visit of representative citizens to Prosecutor Herbert M. Spencer urging that all conceivable angles be exhausted in the still unsolved murder case of David Thompson, one of Spencer's investigators, Vernon L. Anderson, said he could solve the case if he could have Detectives John Glenn and George Sneed assigned to Homicide. [78] However, Chief Michael Morrissey refused this request and as of 1946, the Thompson murder case remained unsolved.[79]

---

[78] "Re-open Unsolved Murder Case", *Indianapolis Recorder* – October 10, 1936, 1,
http://indiamond6.ulib.iupui.edu/cdm/compoundobject/collection/IRecorder/id/23466/rec/1
[79] Opal L. Tandy, "Owl Tavern Hurdles First License Bar", *Indianapolis Recorder* – July 6, 1947, 2,
http://indiamond6.ulib.iupui.edu/cdm/compoundobject/collection/IRecorder/id/93701/rec/59

December 25, 1936

Officers Luster and Davenport Solve a Murder

James Girton

After accusing William Daniel Smith of using crooked dice while gambling, James Girton went home, got a shotgun and then returned to shoot Smith to death.   Without being dispatched on the run, Patrolmen Guy Luster and Spurgeon Davenport, captured James Girton for the murder of Dan Smith, before White officers knew who had committed the crime. [80]

---

[80]   "Dice, Whiskey Held Causes in Yule Slaying", *Indianapolis Recorder* - January 2, 1937, 1,

May 17, 1937

"Cites Alert Cop Whose Coolness Traps Killer"

OFFICER GILBERT JONES

Officer Gilbert Jones was off duty, walking home from a drug store in the evening of May 17, 1937.   He heard screams and the sounds of five gunshots coming from the corner of East and Vermont Streets.   A man ran past him.   Jones, in plain clothes, gave chase.   At New Jersey and

Massachusetts Avenue, the man slowed to a fast walk and Jones caught up to him. Jones asked him "What was that shooting about and what were you doing back there?"

The man had a gun concealed in his coat pocket. He said nothing but struck out at Jones, who struck back, hitting the man on the chin. The man struggled with Jones, then broke loose and moving behind a tree, he pulled a gun and fired at Jones, who took cover behind a parked car. The man fired four shots, striking the car and a telephone pole. Jones returned fire three times and the man fell down. Later examination showed the suspect to be shot in the shoulder, forearm and head. Powder burns on the man's head indicated suicide.

The man was identified as Carl Scroggs and it turned out he had just murdered his wife and son when he encountered Officer Jones. Officer Jones received his second citation in a month. He was highly commended by Lieutenant McCormack, Captain McMurtry and Sergeant Canterbury, firearms expert, who remarked "The shooting was excellent under the circumstances." Jones and Patrolman Spurgeon Davenport had received a commendation on March 10, 1937 from the Chief of Police for their capture of a taxi cab bandit in the act. Several shots were exchanged. [81]

December 18, 1937

Detectives Seize Holdup Men

IPD detectives halted a robbery spree Saturday, December 18th when they captured William Grice and William Brooks. For months, numerous robberies and stick-ups had been occurring in the city of Indianapolis. Six IPD Detectives, George Sneed, Claude White, Gilbert Jones, Ferdinand Holt, Thomas Hopson and John Glenn had concentrated their efforts and two squad cars to solving these crimes.

Detectives Holt, Jones and Hopson were driving through W. St. Clair Street and N. West Street when they saw two men standing in the dark. They backed up to investigate and the men, recognizing them

---

[81] "Cites Alert Cop Whose Coolness Traps Killer", *Indianapolis Recorder* – May 22, 1937, 1,
http://indiamond6.ulib.iupui.edu/cdm/compoundobject/collection/IRecorder/id/54700/rec/1

as police, fled. Gilbert Jones fired a shot which struck Grice in the arm. Jones captured Grice but the other man escaped, as Hopson and Holt couldn't fire at him due to a woman blocking their line of fire.

Later, Detectives Glenn, White and Sneed went to 549 N. Senate Avenue and apprehended Conway. The two suspects admitted to over a dozen robberies and said they were planning on robbing a grocery store when they were apprehended.[82]

December 1937:

IPD Detectives Fred Simon, John Glenn, George Sneed, Claude White and Thomas Hopson receive a written letter of commendation from FBI agent Harold F. Rineicke in December 1937, for their part in assisting in the capture of Luther Benson on October 23, 1937, wanted for murder.[83]

---

[82] "Detectives Seize Holdup Men", *Indianapolis Recorder* – December 25, 1937, 1,
http://indiamond6.ulib.iupui.edu/cdm/compoundobject/collect ion/IRecorder/id/55787/rec/1
[83] "F.B.I. Cites Five Officers Here", *Indianapolis Recorder* – December 25, 1937, 1,
http://indiamond6.ulib.iupui.edu/cdm/compoundobject/collection/IR ecorder/id/55787/rec/1

March 9, 1938:

Partnered with Osa Woodall, Officer Robert "Eddie" Butler left his car having answered a call of a service station robbery at 9th and Capitol Avenue. They saw two suspects run from the door of the station. Butler joined in a lengthy foot pursuit, calling for the suspect to stop. He refused and as the suspect went to jump a fence, Officer Butler fired, striking the suspect. It turned out it was 15-year old Tommy Lee Brown, who Butler thought was a full-grown man in the dark.[84]

---

[84] Opal Tandy, "Officer Fires One Shot To Stop Robbery Suspect" *Indianapolis Recorder* – March 12, 1938, 1, http://indiamond6.ulib.iupui.edu/cdm/compoundobject/collection/IRecorder/id/60453/rec/1

August 6, 1938

Husband Confesses Ax Murder, Arson

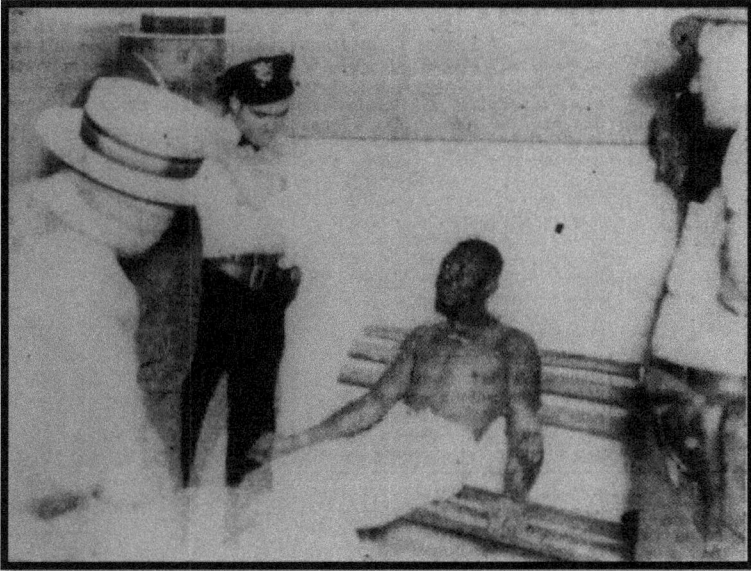

TOP LEFT—The lower part of his body
wrapped in a sheet and the scars left by fire
plainly visible on his arms and body, Jesse
Wilson looks blankly and innocently into
space as Detectives John R. Glenn (Sitting,
in straw hat), George Sneed (standing, in
straw hat), and Deputy Sheriff Tony Maio
(in uniform), Detective Phil Miller (leaning
over), and Deputy Sheriff Max Mieth fire
questions at him in rotation. A few minutes
later, he confessed that he killed his wife

while she dozed off to sleep, with a double-bladed axe then set fire to the bed. [85]

November 19, 1938

Officers Capture Enviable Records

Butler   Davenport   Luster

"They are all three good men and have made outstanding records since they have been connected with the Indianapolis Police Department." These three officers received this citation from the Inspector of Police. These men have shown themselves a credit to the communities in which they work.

[85] "Husband Confesses Ax Murder, Arson", *Indianapolis Recorder* – August 6, 1938, 1, 3,
http://indiamond6.ulib.iupui.edu/cdm/compoundobject/collection/IR ecorder/id/63754/rec/1

[86] IMPD Lichtenberger History Room.

Through their collective efforts five murders, numerous thefts, the saving of lives and many investigations have been handled and cleared with dispatch. When these three youngsters, Guy Luster, Spurgeon Davenport and Robert Butler are sent on a hit they go without delay and usually get their man."[87]

IPD Recruit class appointed January 11, 1938. Known as "The Angels." Clyde Ashby, front row, 2nd from right.

[87] "Officers Capture Enviable Records", *Indianapolis Recorder* – November 19, 1938, 3,
http://indiamond6.ulib.iupui.edu/cdm/compoundobject/collection/IRecorder/id/63992/rec/1

May 1, 1939

1st African-American to be assigned to the IPD Motorcycle Division

The first African-American motorcycle officer in the state of Indiana was appointed May 1, 1939 by IPD Chief of Police Michael Morrissey. Morrissey stated he "wanted to get a man on a cycle for a long time." Officer Guy Luster was chosen for this position. He was a sharpshooter in the Army during WWI and on the police force.

Officer Luster was quoted, "I am grateful for the promotion and I shall work hard to deserve the promotion Chief Morrissey has given me. It is my earnest hope that my work will reflect with the greatest credit upon my efforts and upon the police department. I consider myself fortunate in being selected for this work and my aim will he to do as fine police work as possible, reducing the hazards wherever possible to both motorists and pedestrians, and helping further the outstanding record which my splendid brother officers, and those men who have preceded us, have made."[88]

January 6, 1940:

Bruce P. Robison American Legion Post nominations given to four African-American IPD officers for first time. The annual awards given by the Bruce P. Robinson American Legion Post to Indianapolis police and fire personnel since 1933, were one of the most respected and appreciated awards an IPD officer could receive. For the first time this year, African-Americans were included in the nominations: Officers Gilbert Jones, Alexander Posey, David Clark and Clyde Ashby. None of them won but in future years, IPD officers such as

[88] "Morrissey Names First 'Cycle Traffic Man", *Indianapolis Recorder* – May 6, 1939, 1, http://indiamond6.ulib.iupui.edu/cdm/compoundobject/collection/IRecorder/id/72019/rec/1

Anthony Watkins and Spurgeon Davenport (three time winner), would receive recognition for their fine work. This post was later renamed Robison-Ragsdale.[89]

Also on this date: Eight IPD Acting Detective Sergeants, including Claude C. White, Thomas Hopson and John Glenn were reduced to the rank of Investigator at a salary of $2,100.

April 6, 1940:

A number of African-American officers were reassigned in the first week of April 1940, designed to bolster the IPD Detective Division. Joining Detective Frederick Holt in the Burglary Division were Claude White and Thomas Hopson. Joining Detective George Sneed investigating homicides were Plez Jones and Eddie Butler. Detective John Glenn was then working as a special investigator working on larcenies.[90]

---

[89] "Editor Nominates Five for Legion Merit Awards", *Indianapolis Recorder* – January 6, 1940, 1, http://indiamond6.ulib.iupui.edu/cdm/compoundobject/collection/IRecorder/id/74075/rec/1

[90] "Police Begin New Type Work", *Indianapolis Recorder* – April 6, 1940, 1, http://indiamond6.ulib.iupui.edu/cdm/compoundobject/collection/IRecorder/id/74290/rec/1

October 19, 1940:

Three new African-American men were appointed to the Indianapolis Police Department on October 19, 1940, Grant W. Hawkins, Arthur T. Roney and John Metzger. They were all college graduates, notably, as in those days, few police officers held a degree. The *Indianapolis Recorder* credited Chief Michael F. Morrissey for this move. [91]

February 1941

21 African-Americans now serving with IPD

As of February 1941, there were 21 African-Americans serving on the Indianapolis Police Department. In the first week of February, the administration at IPD made a move directed at the African-American officers, which produced resentment among officers and confusion with the citizenry. Car 31, which had been manned by African-American officers for three years, was now

---

[91] "Three Negroes Added to Police Force", *Indianapolis Recorder* – October 19, 1940, 5,
http://indiamond6.ulib.iupui.edu/cdm/compoundobject/collection/IRecorder/id/89172/rec/1

going to be operated by White officers. The beat covered by Car 31 was bounded by Illinois Street, White River, 10th Street and New York Street. From now on, two African-Americans would be assigned a beat in Car 52 for just one shift, while the rest of the street officers would walk a beat instead of riding.[92] (Car 31 would be restored to African-American officers in January 1943)[93]

Members of an IPD recruit class in 1942 at the target range.

---

[92] "Police Shift Puzzles City", *Indianapolis Recorder* – February 8, 1941, 1,
http://indiamond6.ulib.iupui.edu/cdm/compoundobject/collection/IRecorder/id/90996/rec/1
[93] Opal Tandy, "Bennett Made Detective, Colored in Car 31 Feb 1", *Indianapolis Recorder* – January 23, 1943, 1,
http://indiamond6.ulib.iupui.edu/cdm/compoundobject/collection/IRecorder/id/95523/rec/1

IPD Detective Division, early 1940's. Plez
Jones front row on right.

Here is a summary of their deposition:
Detective Division – 6 men assigned here,
including Sergeant George Sneed.   Since
April of 1940, three men had been assigned
to investigate burglary cases: Detective
Ferdinand Holt, Detective Claude White
and Detective Thomas Hopson. Assigned to
investigate homicides since then were
Sneed, Detective Plez Jones and Detective
Eddie Butler.

---

[94] IMPD Lichtenberger History Room.

Patrolman Fred Starks[95]

Officer Fred Starks – Traffic Station.

Officer Guy Luster – Downtown beat including Indiana Avenue, riding a motorcycle.

---

[95] Indianapolis Childrens Museum Collection.

Officer Jack Hadley with Attucks students, 1941.[96]

Officer Jack Hadley – Traffic officer at 12th & West Streets, near Attucks H.S.

Officer Grant Hawkins and Officer John Metzger – operate Car 52 from 4:30 p.m. to 12:30 a.m. The territory covered by this crew, the only African-Americans in a "prowl" car, was bounded by Tenth Street, Fall Creek Parkway, Illinois Street and White River.

There were then three walking beats, 26, 27 and 28. It was believed this was the first

---

[96] Indianapolis Marion County Library digital archives.

time African-American officers had patrolled these beats.

Boundaries for district 26 were Fall creek and Indiana, New York Street, Blake and Indiana and White river. Boundaries for district 27 were St. Clair, New York, West and Blake. Boundaries for district 28 were St. Clair, New York, Capitol and West. The remaining African-American beat men were:

Officer Arthur Roney
Officer Clyde Ashby
Officer Spurgeon Davenport
Officer David Clark
Officer Osa Woodall
Officer John Coleman
Officer Preston Heater
Officer Roy Kennedy
Officer John Glenn
Officer Norval Bennett

August 29, 1942:

Three African-American IPD officers were credited with the arrests of two youths who had committed numerous crimes. Patrolman Spurgeon Davenport was working a hunch and waited for the two suspects, Charles Douglas, alias "Popeye", age 21 and Charles Mayes, age 20. With the assistance of detectives, Davenport arrested them. They confessed to Davenport and Detective Eddie Butler, of the burglary detail, that they had been committing burglaries for months, splitting hundreds of dollars between them.

The men were held on vagrancy charges until Detective Thomas Hopson could investigate. Hopson and Davenport found several saws, hammers, chisels and other burglar tools in one of their homes. The suspects read off a list of 11 establishments they had burglarized for quick cash. On August 24, 1942, the men were rearrested at the Marion County Jail by Detectives Butler and Hopson and charged with second degree burglary and auto banditry.

Lieutenant Harry Schley, head of the burglary detail recommended that officers Butler, Hopson and Davenport be cited for efficient work and their names listed on the police work bulletin.[97]

---

[97] "Laud 3 Police For Clearing Burglaries", *Indianapolis Recorder* – August 29, 1942, 1,

January 1943

Preston Heater Becomes only African-American Uniform Sergeant

In another IPD shakeup, Preston Heater was promoted to uniform Sergeant, which is a rank an African-American hadn't held on IPD in about a decade (since retirement of Joshua Spearis).   He was chosen to head a 3-man Vice Squad team.   At the same time, Chief Clifford Beeker promoted Officer Norvel Bennett to detective investigator. He was assigned to the homicide detail of the detective force.   This gave IPD seven African American detectives, topping the previous high of six. [98]

March 24, 1943:

Sergeant George Sneed, Officers Plez Jones, Osa Woodall and Norvell Bennett

---

http://indiamond6.ulib.iupui.edu/cdm/compoundobject/collection/IRecorder/id/96551/rec/1

[98]   Opal Tandy, "Bennett Made Detective, Colored in Car 31 Feb 1", *Indianapolis Recorder* – January 23, 1943, 1, http://indiamond6.ulib.iupui.edu/cdm/compoundobject/collection/IRecorder/id/95523/rec/1

were cited by the board of safety for Outstanding and meritorious service. [99]

100

May 11, 1943

IPD Appoints Six African-American Females

---

[99] "Board Cites Sneed, Jones, Woodall, Bennett", *Indianapolis Recorder* – March 27, 1943, 1,
http://indiamond6.ulib.iupui.edu/cdm/compoundobject/collection/IRecorder/id/95674/rec/1
[100] Indianapolis Recorder, September 9, 1944

The Indianapolis Police Department appointed six policewomen on this date who were African-American. They were the first appointed since 1922. In 1944, they were photographed above, left to right: Beatrice Warfield, Georgia Rogers, Sara Mize, Thelma Graves, Ora Phillips. Officer Jacques Durham, standing behind them, taught them proficiency in firearms. [101]

June 12, 1943

14 African-American Officers Added to IPD Manpower

In addition to the six African-American female officers added by IPD, eight male African-American officers were added, which was considered the largest addition at one time of minority hiring in a large American city up to this time.

[101] Six Women Appointed on Local Police Force for Duration", *Indianapolis Recorder* - June 12, 1943, 8, http://indiamond6.ulib.iupui.edu/cdm/compoundobject/collection/IRecorder/id/95859/rec/1

August 21, 1943:

Due to a 1943 Senate Bill #149 passed by the Indiana General Assembly which requires the Indianapolis Police Department to have a number of African-American officers comparable to the radio of African-American citizens, IPD would need to hire 36 additional people of color in the near future. The law made this mandatory. At present, there were 42 African-Americans on the department, men and women. They would have to add 36 to meet the new standards.[102] This goal was not reached.

---

[102]   "Negro Police Must Equal Citizenry Ratio", *Indianapolis Recorder* - August 21, 1943, 1,
http://indiamond6.ulib.iupui.edu/cdm/compoundobject/collection/IRecorder/id/96027/rec/1

November 1943

Preston Heater is first African-American Lieutenant in Uniform Division

Preston Heater   **John R. Glenn**

History was made again under the administration of Chief Clifford Beeker in the promotions of two veteran African-American officers, the week of November 6, 1943. Sergeant Preston Heater, promoted in January of this year to Sergeant in the Uniform Division (the only African-American Sergeant in that division), was promoted to Lieutenant in the Uniform division.

This marked the first time a member of his race had ever held that rank in the Uniform Division. He was also the first African-American to be promoted to Lieutenant since George Sneed in 1925.

Also promoted at this time was John R. Glenn to the rank of Sergeant in the Uniform Division. He joined Jesse Hadley as the 2nd Sergeant in charge of a squad in the Uniform Division. Chief Beeker said these men won their promotions "because of their merit, their long and faithful service in the department and their good records."[103]

---

[103]   "Men Won Promotions – Chief Says", *Indianapolis Recorder* – November 6, 1943, 1, http://indiamond6.ulib.iupui.edu/cdm/compoundobject/collection/IRecorder/id/96214/rec/1

June 6, 1945

African-American Policewoman Assaulted

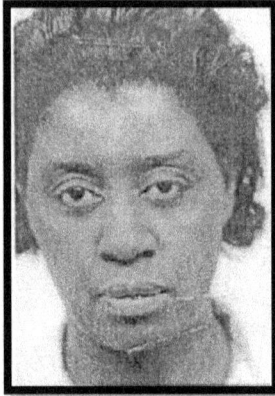

104

Lillian (Woodson) Lewis

105

Juanita Richardson

On June 6, 1945, an incident occurred on a streetcar going west on Washington Street, which became racially charged. It started a White couple, Miss Phyllis Brydon, age 18 and Laron Brydon, age 18, began verbally insulting two African-American IPD policewomen, Juanita Richardson and Lillian (Woodson) Lewis. They persisted in making insulting remarks about them and the IPD administration for hiring African-American policewomen.

---

[104] IMPD Lichtenberger History Room.
[105] IMPD Lichtenberger History Room.

At some point Miss Brydon struck Officer Lewis with a looping right hook to Lewis' jaw while they were on the streetcar. Resenting the brazen insults to the dignity of the positions they held, symbolized by the badges they wore, the policewomen ordered the street car halted and then arrested the couple. They were charged with profanity, resisting arrest and disorderly conduct.

An IPD captain on duty at the time ordered the two policewomen to report to headquarters for a prolonged grilling. Prosecutor Sherwood Blue later had them sign lengthy statements as to what occurred. Members of Judge John L. Niblack's court were mystified as to the actions of the captain and prosecutor, in the absence of any evidence that the two officers did anything other than upholding the law.

The couple requested a change of venue in court.[106]   Unfortunately Officer Lillian Lewis was let go from IPD in June 1946

[106]   "Prosecutor Takes Hand When Women Arrest White Couple", *Indianapolis Recorder* – June 23, 1945, 1, http://indiamond6.ulib.iupui.edu/cdm/compoundobject/collection/IRecorder/id/94551/rec/1

along with Officer Beatrice Garfield.[107]   The Chief of Police Edward D. Rouls had said there were too many policewomen (with the return of IPD officers from WWII service). The African-American community thought they and the other female officers had done an excellent job in preventing juvenile delinquency.

December 29, 1945:

On December 27, 1945, the Board of Public Safety met and promoted Detective Robert Butler and Detective Osa Woodall to the rank of Detective Sergeant in the Detective Department. Police Chief Jesse McMurtry made the announcement, stating that "the promotions were made purely on a merit basis and in recognition of the fine records made by these men." [108]

---

[107]   The Saint, "The Avenoo" *Indianapolis Recorder* – June 29, 1946, 4, second section,
http://indiamond6.ulib.iupui.edu/cdm/compoundobject/collection/IRecorder/id/92889/rec/1
[108]   "Two Win Promotions", *Indianapolis Recorder* - December 29, 1945, 3,
http://indiamond6.ulib.iupui.edu/cdm/compoundobject/collection/IRecorder/id/27523/rec/1

1946:

This is the year Detectives Spurgeon Davenport (left) and James Rogers teamed up and began a long line of arrests and convictions which has been described as unmatched.

April 16, 1947

Six African-American Recruit Officers Appointed

On this date, six WWII veterans were appointed to the Indianapolis Police Department. They were: Chester Coates, David Williams, Luther Kurtz, Charles Jewell, Donald Anderson and Samuel Gibbs.[109]

---

[109]   Opal Tandy, "New Police In Service Six Months", *Indianapolis Recorder* – October 25, 1947, 2, http://indiamond6.ulib.iupui.edu/cdm/compoundobject/collect ion/IRecorder/id/91109/rec/1

Coates   Williams   Kurtz

110

Jewell   Gibbs   Anderson

---

110 IMPD Lichtenberger History Room.

Rookie policewomen are given target practice in February, 1948. On far right is Thelma Sansbury.[111]

---

[111] *The Indianapolis Times*, February 12, 1948.

April 1948

Indianapolis Police Department
Homicide Branch Organized

112

In the first week of April 1948, Lieutenant
Howard Hunter was placed in command of
the newly organized IPD Homicide Bureau.
Twenty men were assigned to him,
including Detective Sergeants Spurgeon
Davenport and James Rogers, African-
Americans. Inspector John J. O'Neal said
he had a high regard for the two men. This
brought Indianapolis up to date with other

---

112 IMPD Lichtenberger History Room.

large cities which had long had such bureaus. [113]

The African-American officers of IPD were aggressive in fighting crime and one example occurred on January 4, 1949. Detective Sergeants John Glenn and Fred Starks were sitting in their squad car in front of the old police headquarters building.

As Starks entered headquarters to report the team ready for duty, he was told by the Captain of Detectives jokingly, "They just sent Car 64 (Homicide Squad) and several police cars to 2418 Columbia Avenue on a murder case. Maybe if you go over there you can solve it for them."

Starks and Glenn saw a number of officers on the scene when they arrived on Columbia Avenue. Major Cook, an 82-year old man had been brutally murdered. No clues or witnesses were readily available. Although not assigned to the case, the following day,

---

[113] "Homicide Bureau Organized in City Police Department", *Indianapolis Recorder* - April 3, 1948, 1, http://indiamond6.ulib.iupui.edu/cdm/compoundobject/collection/IRecorder/id/90016/rec/1

Fred Starks was up before breakfast, walking the streets, showing photos of ex-cons to people while going house to house. When he arrived for work at 4 p.m., he and Sgt. Glenn started the process again, working into the night. Getting a break, they called the Homicide Squad who agreed to raid two homes at once. While Homicide was busy arresting two former roomers at the victim's home, Glenn and Starks walked into an east side restaurant. As they came in, a man began to walk out.

Stopping him, Starks said, "My partner wants to talk to you." Glenn arrested the man, aged 20. By the time 30 minutes had passed, they had recovered a stolen revolver and evidence that linked the 20-year old to the crime scene. He signed a full confession admitting that he had killed the ex-janitor because he refused to let him have money for a trip. He was charged with first degree murder.

For the exceptional detective work the two detectives did over a 60-hour period, Inspector O'Neal and Chief Rouls wrote an inter-departmental commending them, which said in part that they were proud to command and work with men such as Sergeants Glenn and Starks.

Another noteworthy case which occurred in January 1949 started with the death of a would-be bandit who came up second in a pistol duel. The dead man, Daniel S. Madden was taken to the morgue. Detective Sergeant Spurgeon Davenport was phoned at home by Lt. Fae Davis of the Homicide Bureau. It was thought that some of the many victims of robberies that Davenport and his partner Sgt. James Rogers were then investigating should take a look at the dead body.

At 5 p.m. on January 8, 1949, the detectives had a dozen people march past the corpse. At least 10 of them identified Madden as the man who had robbed them. More important to Davenport & Rogers was an unsolved homicide of a man named Andrew Sharpe. The dead suspect Madden had been a suspect in this case. Through extensive leg work and following clues, such as the Madden's revolver which was being tested at police headquarters, and searching a residence he lived in, Sergeants Davenport & Rogers recovered police property which turned out to belong to the murdered Andrew Sharpe. A test bullet fired from Madden's gun matched the one fired into Sharpe's body. This closed out the case.

July 1, 1948

Indianapolis Police Department's Rookie Class

The Indianapolis Police Department's recruit class was held in 1948, being appointed July 1, 1948. They finished their probationary period in 1949. These 1949 photos show some of their activities.[114]

---

[114] *The Indianapolis Star* – July 26, 1949, images from IMPD Historical Photograph Collection.

L-: Sgt. Joseph L. Hunt (right) teaches
firearms training to Rookies Roger N.
Harrison, McClellan and James P. Pearsey

L-R: Harvey G. Foster of the FBI instructs rookies Raymond E. Hutchens, William McClellan and James V. Dabner in firearms proficiency.

1948 IPD Recruit Class[115]
James V. Dabner (far left, front row)
Roger N. Harrison (2nd from left, 2nd row)
Clarence Snorden (3rd from left, 2nd row)
William F. Rapier, (3rd from left, 3rd row)

Above are five African-American rookies
hired during 1948.[116]

---

[115]   Photograph from James P. Pearsey collection.
[116]   "Chief Roul's' Finest", *Indianapolis Recorder* – November
27, 1948, 3,

July 1949

Car 29

A 2nd squad car manned by African-Americans was added in July 1949. It patrolled a racially mixed area which was bounded roughly by 16th Street, north to 32nd Street, south to Montcalm and Harding Streets, West to Capitol Avenue. The first African-American officers assigned to this car included: John Metzger, John Bailey, Bailey Coleman, William Rapier, and Albert Booth and James V. Dabner. This area had previously been patrolled by White officers. [117]

http://indiamond6.ulib.iupui.edu/cdm/compoundobject/collection/IRecorder/id/89708/rec/1

[117] Opal L. Tandy, "The Avenoo", *Indianapolis Recorder* – July 16, 1949, 12,
http://indiamond6.ulib.iupui.edu/cdm/compoundobject/collection/IRecorder/id/88094/rec/1

November 26, 1949:

For several weeks in the fall of 1949, the Indianapolis Police Department had been searching for a White man wearing a polka-dot mask and armed with two guns, who had committed a series of robberies. Although not assigned to this case, Detectives Spurgeon Davenport and James Rogers "got a line" on Fred Bean, age 26, who they felt was the suspect in these crimes.

After questioning their suspect Fred Bean, he admitted to getting approximately $5,000 in 20 robberies, including some in Anderson and Evansville, Indiana. Davenport and Rogers revealed Bean as the culprit, an African-American man with a light complexion instead of the "White" man IPD had been searching for. In connection to this case, Officers Clyde Ashby and James Dabner of Squad 20 arrested Claude Fingers, who participated in four of the robberies. [118]

---

[118] "Good Police Work Leads To 'Busy' Hold-Up Man's Arrest", *Indianapolis Recorder* – November 26, 1949, 1,

March 18, 1950:

In March of 1950, IPD employed 15 policewomen. Four were African-American. They were assigned to the Juvenile Aid Division, as were many policewomen at that time. They were described by their supervisor, Lt. Forrest Higgs as "exceptionally-good workers." Pictured left to right with Lt. Higgs are: Mrs. Sarah Mize Jones, Mrs. Georgia Rogers, Mrs. Thelma Graves, and Mrs. Thelma Sansbury. [119]

---

http://indiamond6.ulib.iupui.edu/cdm/compoundobject/collect
ion/IRecorder/id/88417/rec/1

[119] "Police Dept., JAD, Now Ably Served by Women",
Indianapolis Recorder – March 18, 1950, 1,
http://indiamond6.ulib.iupui.edu/cdm/compoundobject/collect
ion/IRecorder/id/88917/rec/1

The article accompanying this picture in the March 18, 1950 issue of the *Indianapolis Recorder* profiled the four currently serving African-American policewomen. Officers Rogers, Jones and Graves were appointed as emergency manpower in May 1943. Officer Sansbury was appointed in 1947. These women worked in pairs, as did male officers at that time, Mrs. Rogers and Mrs. Jones as one team, Mrs. Graves and Mrs. Sansbury as another.

Their 8-hour day started by reporting to the Juvenile Aid Division to receive their assignments and interviewing children if necessary. The types of duties they performed sounded very similar to those of Emma Baker and Mary Mays in 1918-1922. Checking taverns, theatres and other places for delinquents. They covered all of Indianapolis instead of one beat and called headquarters every hour to see if any new assignments had come in. Within a few years, most IPD policewomen were reduced to the roll of secretaries, so these women were performing a unique role for that time.

July 13, 1950

Police Officers Cited for Outstanding Work

Lieutenant George Sneed and Sergeant Alexander Posey captured Bennie Gilmer, a suspect in the burglary of Clark's Auto Wash, 112 N. Meridian Street. Within a few minutes of the burglary, armed with only a brief suspect description over the radio, Sneed and Posey spotted him at 10th and Illinois Streets. They brought Gilmer to the scene of the crime where he was identified as the burglar. They also recovered the stolen merchandise and money. Chief Edward D. Rouls commended both of them "for their observation and initiative in the apprehension." Marking his 30th year with IPD, Lieutenant Sneed was still one of the best detectives within IPD. [120]

---

[120] "Police Officers Cited for Outstanding Work", *Indianapolis Recorder* – July 22, 1950, 1,
http://indiamond6.ulib.iupui.edu/cdm/compoundobject/collection/IRecorder/id/91468/rec/1

June 26, 1951

"Mad Dog" Husband Kills Officer; Wounds Another

Clarence Snorden[121] Thomas Williams

Another in a long line of tragedies within the Indianapolis Police Department began on June 26, 1951 when a man called IPD headquarters. The first call was ignored, the second said, "Come to 227 W. 14th Street, a man has been killed." In fact at this time, no one had been killed, but the man living at that address, later identified

---

[121] IPD History: In Memorium,
http://www.indy.gov/eGov/City/DPS/IMPD/About/Memoriam/Pages/csnorden.aspx

as James Hoard, made the calls after threatening his wife, "When they hit that gate, I'm going to shoot them, then they'll kill me."

IPD dispatched Car 29, manned by Officers Thomas Williams and Clarence Snorden to the run. Arriving at 10:30 p.m., the officers got out of the car, unaware that Hoard was sitting in his darkened house, holding a shotgun.

Snorden was the first officer out of the car and was looking for the house number with his flashlight when Hoard fired his shotgun through the front door glass. The .12-gauge charge struck Officer Snorden in the chest. He fell forward on his face, gun still in his holster.
Officer Williams had almost reached his partner when another shotgun blast was fired, which struck him in the face and forehead. Rushed to General Hospital, Clarence Snorden died about an hour later, while Thomas Williams was in critical condition.

Interviewed at headquarters later by Detective Sergeants Bethel Gaither and

James Gaughan, the wife of the gunman, Mary Hoard explained that the situation started when she informed her husband that she was leaving him due to the abuse she had received during their marriage. He was threatening suicide and got his shotgun before her brother could. Hoard then set up his ambush. After shooting Snorden, he said "I killed him". Hoard then pointed the shotgun at his chest and blew a large hole through it, committing suicide.

After the officers were shot, Sergeants Gaither and Gaughan arrived seconds later from the Homicide Division, followed by Sergeant Clinton Auter. After seeing Snorden's lighted flashlight laying in the yard, they realized the two officers had been shot.

Gaither and Gaughan crawled to them and pulled their bodies away from the home. Sergeant Auter began firing into the house as they did. Sergeant Gaither called for assistance and then the three officers poured round after round of shotgun fire into the house, not realizing the suspect was already dead. Eventually Gaither made his way into the home, saw the dead body of the suspect and called a halt to the shooting.

Officer Thomas Williams

Officer Thomas Williams was blinded in his right eye and almost lost an arm due to his severe wounds. However, he survived to return to duty and spent many years serving the citizens of Indianapolis. [122] Officer Snorden had served with the Indianapolis Police Department for three years and was a World War II veteran. He

---

[122] "Mad Dog" Husband Kills Officer; Wounds Another", *Indianapolis Recorder* – June 30, 1951,.1, http://indiamond6.ulib.iupui.edu/cdm/compoundobject/collect ion/IRecorder/id/85607/rec/1

was survived by his expectant wife and a 22-month-old son.

January 1952

The McCrimmon Case – Part II

George McCrimmon, who had escaped from the Marion County Jail in 1936, vowing to kill IPD Detectives George Sneed and Ferdinand Holt, escaped by walking out of a municipal court room in Indianapolis, in January 23, 1952. This was his four escape in 18 years. He had broken out of a Columbus, Ohio jail on January 15th. His previous escapes were in 1933 and the aforementioned 1936.

It was revealed that when he was sentenced in 1936 to a 10-25 year term in prison, he had told the police that he and three other men planned on stealing guns from the armory at New Albany, hold up an Indianapolis bank and kill the two police sergeants who had arrested him previously (Sneed and Holt). Ironically, it was one of those men, now Lieutenant George Sneed, who arrested George McCrimmon on January 22, 1952 while he was on the run after escaping from Columbus, Ohio.[123]   He still considered McCrimmon a very dangerous individual.

George McCrimmon was finally apprehended May 14, 1952 by two IPD detectives.

IPD Recruit class appointed November 22, 1950. African-American recruits are William Bryant (top row, far right) and Leon Chisley, (middle row, far right).

---

[123] "Authorities Set Up Dragnet for Slippery Fugitive", The Vidette Messenger, Valparaiso, Indiana - January 24, 1952, 5, Ancestry.com. The Vidette Messenger (Valparaiso, Indiana) [database on-line]. Provo, UT, USA: Ancestry.com Operations Inc, 2005.

May 6, 1953

Four Police Get Permanent Rank

Clockwise, L-R: Coates, Davenport, Glenn, Jones.

On this date, 78 IPD officers were promoted to permanent "merit" ranks. Included were four African-American men. Spurgeon Davenport was promoted from acting

Lieutenant to merit Lieutenant. He finished first in his division in the officer's school in July 1952. Davenport always believed in applying himself on promotional exams.

Permanent rank of detective sergeant was given to acting detectives Garland Jones, Chester Coates and John Glenn.

Det. Sgt. James Rogers, the other member of the celebrated team of Indianapolis detectives, Davenport and Rogers, was granted permanent rank in the fall of 1952. He also finished in the last officers' school with highest grades.

"Lt. Davenport expects to enter the next school this July to qualify for rank of captain. Sgts. Rogers, Glenn and Coates are expected to make the bid for promotions to lieutenant. The granting of permanent ranks to Indianapolis police officers is in line with a campaign pledge by Mayor Alex Clark to improve the moral of the department by giving the greatest incentives and security to its members" said the *Indianapolis Recorder.* [124]

July 15, 1953

Two Policewomen assigned to Detective Division

[125]

Thelma Graves   Ella Coleman

In a bold move forward, Inspector Noel Jones of the Detective Division requested two African-American policewomen be transferred from the Juvenile Aid Division to the center detail of his division.

---

[124] "Four Police Get Permanent Rank", *Indianapolis Recorder* – May 9, 1953, 1,
http://indiamond6.ulib.iupui.edu/cdm/compoundobject/collection/IRecorder/id/31774/rec/1
[125] IMPD Lichtenberger History Room.

131

Patrolwomen Thelma Graves and Ella Coleman were the officers selected. "I am sure they will be an asset to our division", Inspector Jones remarked Wednesday. He continued that this was the latest in a series of manpower moves to "fully utilize the services of the best officers in the department."

Inspector Noel Jones, 1952.[126]

The center detail of the detective division mainly involved the shoplift detail in downtown department stores. Ella Coleman spent most of her career in this area.

---

[126] IMPD Lichtenberger History Room.

Inspector Noel Jones had first assigned Detective Sergeants John Glenn and Garland Jones to the Homicide & Robbery Division. Anthony Watkins and Samuel Gibbs were then moved from the uniform division to the center detail as a special narcotics team a few weeks earlier. Up to this time, African-American policewomen had been assigned to the Juvenile Aid Division.[127]

October 9,1953

Officers Make Indianapolis' 1st Civil Rights Violation Arrest

On Friday, October 9th, Officer John T. Bailey and his rookie partner Hardister Buckner went into Weiss' Delicatessen, 23 E. Market Street just after noon. The counterman filled their order and was about to hand it to them so they could get a seat and eat when the owner, Lee Levengood, 39, interrupted by saying "THAT FOOD GOES OUT." After being told the officers

---

[127] "Two Policewomen Given Different Duties", *Indianapolis Recorder* – July 18, 1953, 1, http://indiamond6.ulib.iupui.edu/cdm/compoundobject/collection/IRecorder/id/32032/rec/1

intended to eat inside by the counterman, the owner replied, "We don't serve colored in here", referring to the officers.

Officer Bailey told the owner that he had eaten inside this restaurant previously. Levengood replied "If I had know about it, you wouldn't have!" and refused to serve them.

John T. Bailey   Hardister Buckner

The officers arrested Levengood for violation of the Indiana Civil Rights Law, believed to be the first time someone had been arrested on the spot and jailed for violating this law, which hadn't been enforced.   At a preliminary hearing, the Henry J. Richardson Jr., of the national legal staff of the NAACP, represented the officers, as a friend to the court.

Levengood's attorney attempted to get a 30 day continuance, since the charge was a misdemeanor "of no consequence and doesn't mean anything." "A man's civil rights mean a whole lot", replied Judge Scott McDonald firmly. [128]

In November 1953, a jury deliberated 2 hours before finding in favor of the defendant in the case.

Another such incident occuring during this era happened when several IPD homicide detectives went to get something to eat after working on a case. They were White except for Lt. Spurgeon Davenport. The waitress came to took their order, saying "I can serve all of you except *him*."

One of the White detectives said, "Well, if you're not serving him, you're not serving any of us" and they got up and left.[129]

---

[128] "Jimcrowed Cops Jail Café Owner", *Indianapolis Recorder* – October 17, 1953, 1, http://indiamond6.ulib.iupui.edu/cdm/compoundobject/collection/IRecorder/id/31156/rec/1

[129] Story related by Lt. James P. Pearsey who worked Homicide 1952-1956.

December 5, 1953:

THIS WAR IS OVER: Apparently believing in preparedness, a gang of hoodlums who police say are responsible for a large number of robberies and burglaries, scooped up this assortment of firearms during a burglary but it didn't get very far. Det. Lt. Spurgeon Davenport and Sgt. John Glenn, shown above examining the captured arms, took weapons from the trunk of a car in which they arrested Wayman Kimball and Charles Johnson. Harold Brown and. George Higgins were later arrested. Detectives believe the quartet is responsible for many holdups of liquor stores and neighborhood grocery stores. Sgt. Glenn (right) is holding a vicious-looking sawed-off shotgun reportedly used by members of the gang in holdups. (*RECORDER* PHOTO by Jim Cummings.) The *Indianapolis Recorder* – December 5, 1953 [130]

IPD Recruit class appointed January 5, 1953. Includes Hardister Buckner, James Mitchell, Clarence White & Phillip Parker.

---

[130] "Nab 4 'Sawed-Off Shotgun' Bandits", *Indianapolis Recorder* – December 5, 1953, 1, http://indiamond6.ulib.iupui.edu/cdm/compoundobject/collection/IRecorder/id/31275/rec/1

IPD Recruit Class – Photo Dated April 15, 1954.[131]

Two of the three female recruits were Sarah Lee Jones and Emily C. Weathers.

---

[131] IMPD Lichtenberger History Room.

June 9, 1954

Police Sergeants Given Permanent Rank

Six veteran African-American officers were to the merit rank of Sergeant on this date. They were Plez Jones, Fred Starks, Osa Woodall, Thomas Williams, Claude White and Robert Butler. All but Thomas Williams held the rank of Acting Sergeant.[132]

June 27, 1954

Major Undercover Operation Nets "Most Wanted" Burglar

The Indianapolis Police Department detective bureau had been in pursuit of a team of professional burglars in 1954 and they set in motion a major undercover operation in order to capture them. Inspector Noel Jones, head of the bureau and Lieutenant Arthur Ratz, head of the burglary detail, set up a plan where all the

---

[132] "Police Sgts. Given Permanent Rank", *Indianapolis Recorder* – June 12, 1954, 1, http://indiamond6.ulib.iupui.edu/cdm/compoundobject/collection/IRecorder/id/33492/rec/1

detective cars were painted conventional colors and the long radio aerials were removed. Detective Sergeants James Rogers and Robert "Eddie" Butler were assigned to tail the suspects and keep headquarters informed of their movements.

When it was realized additional manpower was needed, Officers John Glenn, Anthony Watkins and Samuel Gibbs were assigned. These five officers kept the burglary gang under almost constant surveillance. Their quarry was Charles Willie Mays, 33, rated by detectives as one of the best safe-men in town.

For some time, the detectives maintained this surveillance, knowing that at times Mays' gang was committing burglaries but not having enough evidence to take it to court. In order to force the gang's hand, IPD had local finance companies repossess their cars and put them on foot, so they would be desperate for cash. This resulted in the gang making a foolish burglary attempt.

On Sunday, June 27, 1954, the gang had been followed for several hours by IPD detectives before they entered the Cloverleaf Creameries, 1417 N. Harding Street. Across the street, 3,000 fans were watching the Indianapolis Indians play at Victory Field.

Inspector Jones, Lieutenant Ratz, Sergeant Glenn and Sergeant Michael Garvey watched as the men entered the creamery and waited for them to emerge. When a driver for the creamery went to the front door and shook it, Mays and his gang fled, having gotten the safe as far as the door. They got into a car owned by one of the gang but were surrounded before they could start the motor.

Charles W. Mays, along with Eugene H. Freeman, 33 and Maurice Anderson, 20, were arrested. Mays was believed to have taken part in a burglary of the L. S. Ayres warehouse shortly before Christmas 1953 in which $6,000 was taken. Two Omar Baking Company jobs reportedly netted him and his gang $15,000 in November 1953. A $10,000 Rose Time Company burglary was credited to him, along with numerous other burglaries.[133]

July 24, 1954:

EXAMINE CAPTURED ARTILLERY: Policewomen Thelma Sansbury (left) and Emily Weathers are examining a rifle and a pistol they recovered when they cracked a six-member teenage burglary gang. In all

---

[133] "Most Wanted Burglar Leads Two Pals into Police Net", *Indianapolis Recorder* - July 3, 1954, 2, http://indiamond6.ulib.iupui.edu/cdm/compoundobject/collection/IRecorder/id/33543/rec/1

two rifles and four revolvers were uncovered and seven burglaries clear up. (*Recorder* Photo by Jim Cummings.) [134]

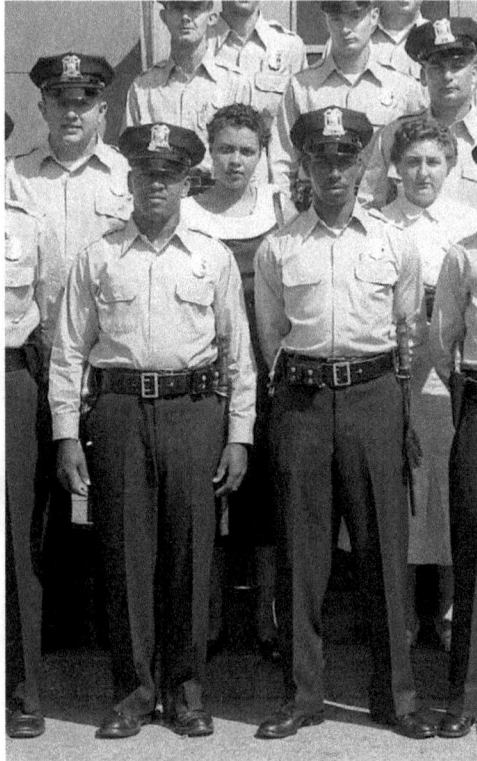

IPD Recruit class appointed June 20, 1955. African-American members included Policewoman Barbara Sneed.

---

[134] "Examine Captured Artillery", *Indianapolis Recorder* – July 24, 1954, 1, http://indiamond6.ulib.iupui.edu/cdm/compoundobject/collection/IRecorder/id/33594/rec/1

July 26, 1954

Five men engage 75 IPD officers in gun battle after aborted holdup

Officer Oscar B. Donahue leads suspect
Jerry Martin, 29 to jail.[135]

---

[135]   WIRE Photo in possession of author.

On July 26, 1954, five men held up the Best Finance Company.

IPD interrupted them and in the brief gun battle which followed, Detective Joseph Chestnut was shot in the ankle and four of the suspects were captured. Patrolman Oscar B. Donahue was singled out for praise by fellow officers and newsmen for the efficient way he relayed communications from headquarters to Lieutenant Joseph Klein in charge of 75 officers on the scene. [136]

January 9, 1955:

Sergeant Thomas Williams leads a raid on a private poker game at 543 W. Michigan Street. His team included Officers Albert Sheridan, Thelma Donahue, William Rapier and William Rowe. This is noteworthy for the participation of a female officer. [137]

---

[136] "Ability Pays Off", *Indianapolis Recorder* – July 31, 1954, 1, http://indiamond6.ulib.iupui.edu/cdm/compoundobject/collection/IRecorder/id/33611/rec/1

[137] "State and Local Officials Drive To Hit Gamblers", *Indianapolis Recorder* – January 15, 1955, 1, http://indiamond6.ulib.iupui.edu/cdm/compoundobject/collection/IRecorder/id/34894/rec/1

July 2, 1955

Officer Emily Weathers Participates in Drug Raid

Emily Weathers

On July 2, 1955, two teams of IPD officers raided the barber shop of Herman Lopez Redd, age 31 and his home at the same time. While Detective Sergeant Anthony Watkins' team raided the barber shop, Detective Sergeant William Owen and his team, including Patrolwoman Emily C. Weathers, raided the home, located at 2070 Highland Avenue.

There they found Laura Redd and a supply of heroin and drug paraphernalia. Sgt. Watkins team consisted of veteran

Detective Sergeant Fred Starks, Patrolman William Cobb and Patrolman William Parker.[138]

July 4, 1955

Two Policewomen Chase Down Shoplifter

Thelma Graves   Ella Coleman

On the same week that Policewomen Sarah Lee Jones had to draw her weapon (see below), two of her fellow female officers,

---

[138] "Barber, 2 Men Nabbed in 2 Dope Raids", *Indianapolis Recorder* – July 9, 1955, 1-2,
http://indiamond6.ulib.iupui.edu/cdm/compoundobject/collection/IRecorder/id/36963/rec/1

both African-American made news. A man who had jumped bond in Texas on an armed robbery charge, walked out of a downtown J.C. Penney department store without paying for a briefcase. He was spotted by IPD Policewomen Thelma Graves and Ella Coleman, who were assigned to watch for such incidents at downtown department stores.

The officers attempted to question the man, later identified as George Drummond, age 42, but he bolted, running around Monument Circle, into an alley north of Penney's, where Graves and Coleman cornered him. They told him to sit down and he responded by throwing a box at Officer Coleman and took off again.

They gave chase, down Ohio Street, through a tavern and back into the alley, where Officer Coleman fired two shots into the air and Drummond fell flat onto his face. The man had $2,600 in his wallet. He was found to be wanted on the Texas warrant. [139]

---

[139]   "Policewomen's Speed, Grit, Too Much For Thief", *Indianapolis Recorder* – July 9, 1955, 5,

July 9, 1955

Policewomen Join in Crackdown on Bootleg Taxicabs

Sarah Lee Jones

The Indianapolis Police Department had an ongoing war against unlicensed, or "bootleg" taxicabs in the 1950's. In 1955, a team of officers, Policewoman Thelma Donahue, Officer William Rapier and Officer William Rowe made 115 arrests in this effort. Donahue and Rapier were African-American. During the first week of July, 1955, this team was replaced by Policewomen Sarah Lee Jones and Overa Ward and Officer Leon Chisley.

During the first six days on the job, the new IPD team made nine arrests of bootleg cabbies. Policewoman Sarah Lee Jones was forced to draw her weapon on Roy Woods, 26. She got into his car at 23rd and Martindale, directing him to the 2500 block of Guilford Avenue, where Officer Chisley was waiting. As the cabbie pulled up on Guilford Avenue, he recognized Chisley and sped off with Jones in the car. He tried to push Officer Sarah Lee Jones out of the car and she pulled her gun. Woods skidded to a stop and got out and ran, later giving himself up.

Policewoman Emily C. Weathers was injured in a car chase of another bootleg cabbie a few months after this incident.[140]

---

[140] "Arrest Nine in War on Bootleg Taxicabs", *Indianapolis Recorder* – July 9, 1955, 5,
http://indiamond6.ulib.iupui.edu/cdm/compoundobject/collection/IRecorder/id/36963/rec/1

July 9, 1955

IPD Continues War on Heroin Trafficking in Indianapolis

Ella C. Coleman

Fred Swego

On July 9, 1955, IPD launched a raid on a woman from Chicago who was an admitted prostitute and a major drug dealer. This raid was conducted by Narcotics Bureau members Detective Sergeants William Owens and Fred Swego along with Policewoman Ella Coleman. For four months, Sergeant Owen and the other members of the Narcotics Bureau, Detective Sergeants Anthony Watkins, J. Sammuel

Gibbs and Robert Keithley, had conducted surveillance on the woman and her regular trips to Chicago to deliver dope to Indianapolis. Police found 300 grains of heroin in a suitcase in her room, valued at over $1,000.

The woman, identified as Gladys Anderson, age 27, boasted of earning $100 a customer from prostitution activities. She got 90 days in prison and a fine of $100 and costs on Monday. William Owen rated this as a major arrest. [141]

---

[141] "Chicago Woman, Arrested Here With Dope, Arrested", *Indianapolis Recorder* – July 16, 1955, 1, http://indiamond6.ulib.iupui.edu/cdm/compoundobject/collection/IRecorder/id/36980/rec/1

August 2, 1955

Officer Emily Weathers Assists in another Narcotics Raid

    The IPD Narcotics Bureau struck once again, on August 2, 1955, with a raid on a woman described as "Indianapolis' biggest dope dealer." This was Geraldine Rutledge, age 28, 928 Paca. Armed with a federal search warrant, federal agent William F. Penberthy, along with IPD officers Detective Sergeants William Owens and Robert E. Keithley, and Policewoman Emily Weathers, confiscated 33 heroin capsules and a package of 50 grains of heroin.

Earning between $500 and $1000 a week from her drug trafficking, Rutledge was making two to three trips to Chicago a week to get more drugs for distribution, since IPD knocked off her competitors, including Herman Redd on July 2nd.[142]

November 19, 1955

Chief John Ambuhl

IPD Chief of Police Discusses Integration of Department

---

[142] "Woman 'Biggest Dope Dealer'", *Indianapolis Recorder* – August 6, 1955, 8, http://indiamond6.ulib.iupui.edu/cdm/compoundobject/collection/IRecorder/id/35081/rec/1

[143] IMPD Lichtenberger History Room.

In an interview, outgoing IPD Chief of Police John E. Ambuhl readily admitted that the police department was segregated but refused to answer questions about possible changes to the racial structure. He said as he was leaving his position those questions were best answered by his successor. He was due to be demoted as Phil Bayt was elected Mayor the previous week.

Chief Ambuhl said that although he was not himself in favor of integration, the department needed more African-American officers. As it was currently set up, IPD could not be integrated until it was able to hire more African-American officers. "We simply do not have enough Negro officers to do the job as the department is currently set up. And if we integrated, we'd have to have more colored officers. As it is now, we don't have much choice where we'll put Negro officers to work."

He continued, "There are things Negro officers can get that no white man can and we have to use our officers in the most effective manner." At present, most African-American officers were assigned around the Indiana Avenue area.

Chief Ambuhl said he was in favor of hiring any African-American officers who could qualify for the department.

Admitting that the department would be integrated "sooner or later", he noted the effectiveness of integration in the IPD Narcotics squad, which consisted of three white men and two African-Americans. It had made great strides in restricting drug trafficking since being formed in 1953. There had been a push by the *Indianapolis Recorder* to integrate the IPD Homicide Division, which in November 1955 was totally white. Homicide investigators were complaining that they can't get cooperation from African-Americans and as a result, could not get sufficient evidence to get convictions from the prosecutor's office.

There was a growing problem of murder in the African-American community, 22 of 27 murders in 1955 being committed by African-Americans. Chief Ambuhl promised to assign African-American detectives to the next murder case where an

African-American is principally involved.
144

Car 27

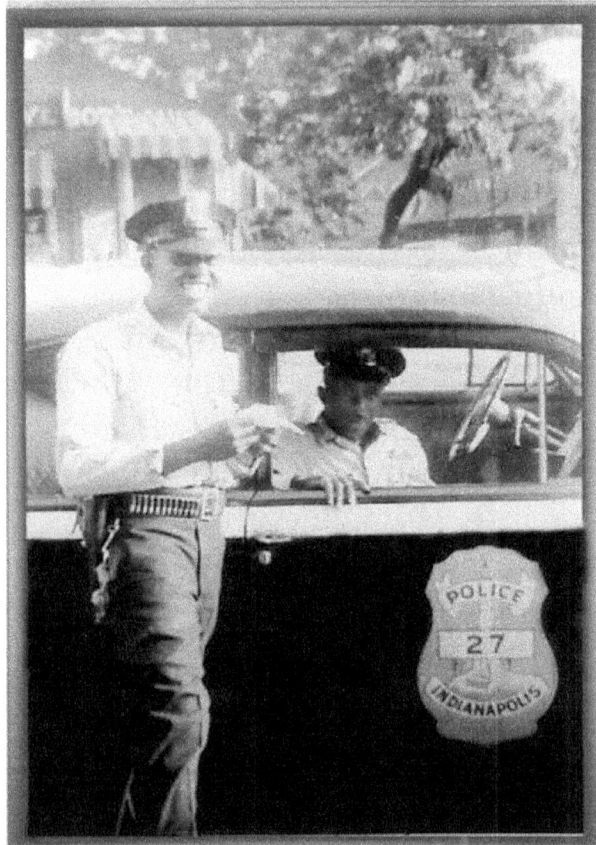

Patrolman Clarence A. White (standing) &
Alfred Finnell, (sitting), Car 27.[145]

---

[144] Jim Cummings, "Chiefs Balk at Integration", *Indianapolis Recorder* – November 19, 1955, 1,
http://indiamond6.ulib.iupui.edu/cdm/compoundobject/collection/IRecorder/id/35912/rec/1
[145] IMPD Lichtenberger History Room.

"Car 27" was the number assigned to an IPD squad car that was designated for African-American officers to patrol the near west side of Indianapolis in. The earliest mentions of Car 27 in the *Indianapolis Recorder* come in 1943, when Patrolmen Spurgeon Davenport and Jacque Durham rode in it. The list of men who were assigned in this car through 1962 after which it was apparently integrated is too long to show except for the men who spent multiple years in. This includes

James V. Dabner (1951-54)
Alfred Finnell (1951-1957)
Charles Jewell (1947-1951)
Oscar Donahue (1954-1956)
James Gaines (1954-1956)

Car 27 – L-R: Thomas Williams, Thomas Bryant and Chester Coates.

The boundaries that Car 27 patrolled were altered during day shift and night shift. During the day, it lay between Michigan and 16th streets and the White River and Illinois Street. At night, the north-south boundary was reduced further to between 10th Street and Fall Creek, a distance of about a dozen blocks.

Car 27, 1946.[146]

There were racial implications to this, White citizens not feeling comfortable it is thought, with African-American officers patrolling their neighborhoods at night.[147] The policy of restricting African-American officers to areas where African-Americans predominately lived, started in 1876, would exist until the early 1960's.

---

[146] IMPD Lichtenberger History Room.
[147]   James Patterson, "You Have to Live Above Racism- Former IPD Captain", *Indianapolis Recorder* - April 1, 2010, http://www.indianapolisrecorder.com/news/features/article_7 5e9c977-c7be-5e01-a060-f15e671df553.html

March 1956

Two African-Americans assigned to new IPD Narcotics Bureau

Albert Booth   Anthony Watkins

In March of 1956, the Indianapolis Police Department organized a Narcotics Bureau for the first time. Four men were handpicked, including African-Americans Detective Sergeant Anthony Watkins and Detective Sergeant Albert Booth. The other two men picked were Detective Sergeant Robert Keithley and Detective Sergeant William Owen. [148]

---

[148] Jim Cummings, "New Dope Law Works Magic", *Indianapolis Recorder* - March 10, 1956, 1,
http://indiamond6.ulib.iupui.edu/cdm/compoundobject/collect
ion/IRecorder/id/28990/rec/2

March 2, 1956

IPD Detectives Recapture Escaped Prisoners

Two IPD detectives played a primary role in the recapture of three ex-convicts. John Bingham, age 22 and Robert Allen Walker, age 31, had overpowered two deputy sheriffs, taking their guns, then escaping from the dental clinic of General Hospital, where they had been taken. They were joined by Emmett Ard, age 28. This ignited an intense manhunt for hours.
At 12th and Missouri Streets the night of the escape, Detective Sergeant Anthony Watkins and Detective Sergeant Albert Booth spotted Bingham and Walker.

The officers jumped out of their car, guns drawn and ordered the fugitives to halt. Bingham threw his hands up but Walker, gun in hand, ran. Albert Booth, the best shot on IPD, fired once and Watkins fired twice. Walker disappeared. He gave himself up at IPD Headquarters Saturday night, March 3, 1956. He had bullet wounds in the shoulder and leg which he said were received the night the officers fired at him.[149]

June 23, 1956

Two IPD Detectives Shot

On the evening of Saturday, June 23, 1956, two ex-convicts named Samuel W. Woodson, age 33 and Ivo E. Harding, age 24, held up the Bell-Air Drive-in at Kentucky and Tibbs Avenues. Woodson drove up to the ticket office, got out and held a gun on the cashier as Harding cleaned out the cash register. As they drove past Kentucky and Morris, State Trooper Gerald D. Curts flagged them down.

As Curts unfastened his seat belt, Woodson approached the side of his car and put his gun in the trooper's face, ordering him to put his gun on the seat. He picked the gun up and ordered the trooper to drive on, firing several shots at it as he drove away, one going through the rear window.

---

[149] Commend Officers in Recapture of Ex-Convicts", *Indianapolis Recorder* – March 10, 1956, 1, http://indiamond6.ulib.iupui.edu/cdm/compoundobject/collection/IRecorder/id/28990/rec/2

They shot and wounded IPD Detective Sergeant Fred Whisler and Detective Sergeant John T. Morris as they tried to question Woodson. These officers were in fair condition in General Hospital June 28th. When brought into headquarters, African-American Detective Sergeant James Rogers, original member of the Homicide and Robbery Detail, got confessions from the suspects June 24th after a long period of questioning from top IPD brass, in which the men remained tight lipped. Rogers and his partner, Lt. Spurgeon Davenport remained in the interview room after the brass departed and Harding was the first to crack under Roger's skillful questioning.[150]

---

[150] "Hold 2 Ex-Convicts in Shooting of Detectives", *Indianapolis Recorder* – June 30, 1956, 1, http://indiamond6.ulib.iupui.edu/cdm/compoundobject/collection/IRecorder/id/29500/rec/1

July 14, 1956

Records Support Promotions of Three Officers

Clockwise, L-R: Anthony Watkins, Oscar Donahue, Roger Harrison

The Board of Safety made a major move by promoting three veteran African-American officers. They were:

Anthony Watkins, promoted from Detective Sergeant to Lieutenant. A member of IPD since 1944, he joined Spurgeon Davenport as the highest African-Americans at that rank on the department. He was director of the Lockfield PAL Club in the mid-1940's, served as a narcotics detective and also did patrol duty. He received commendations in 1949 and 1952 for his efficient work. He also solved a hit and run fatality and a wave of mail box thefts.

Oscar Donahue, promoted from Patrolman to Sergeant. Donahue joined IPD in 1943 and during the year 1954-55, he and partner James Gaines captured 15 holdup men. In 1955, he disarmed a holdup man who had a gun trained on Patrolman Thomas Hodges. He earned the Robinson-Ragsdale award in 1953.

Roger Harrison, promoted from Patrolman to Sergeant. Harrison was appointed to the force July 1, 1948 and served practically the entire time in a squad car. He was commended in April and May of 1950 for his apprehension of two holdup men and "good police work and devotion to duty while under fire in the capture of a liquor store hold- up man."

All three officers would start their new assignments as uniform officers in the Indiana Avenue area.[151]

Members of the recruit class appointed May 22, 1957. African-American members included Alonzo Watford, George Lewis and Richard Collins.

---

[151] "Records Support Promotions of Three Officers", *Indianapolis Recorder* – July 14, 1956, 1, http://indiamond6.ulib.iupui.edu/cdm/compoundobject/collection/IRecorder/id/29075/rec/1

November 11, 1956

Ace Detectives Solve Murder of U.S. Army Officer

Top:L-R: Lt. Davenport & Sgt. Rogers.
Bottom: Sgt. Glenn, Sgt. Jones

One of the most sensational murder cases in Indianapolis history occurred November 11,

1956. On that date, U.S. Army Lieutenant
Phillip Glessner, age 24 and Miss Barbara
Winders, age 21, were sitting in his parked
car near E. 23rd Street.   Four men driving
west on 23rd Street spotted them and
decided on a robbery.

Two of the four, who were both armed, crept
up on either side of the car. As stated later
by one of the suspects, when Miss Winder
spotted him, she screamed and grabbed his
gun, which went off. The shot struck
Lieutenant Glessner in the head.   The shot
entered the right side of his head, traveling
to the left side.

Although he was treated for the wound, the
soldier died on Wednesday, November 14th.
Assigned to this important case were
Lieutenant Spurgeon Davenport and
Detective Sergeants James Rogers, John
Glenn and Garland Jones.

With few clues, the detectives spent almost
a solid week investigating the murder.
They had one lead, a palm print on a soft
drink bottle found in an abandoned car.
This print was traced to James Edward
Smith, age 20, who was arrested Friday,

November 16th.   This arrest led to the
rapid apprehension of James' brother
Thomas Eugene Smith, 18, William D.
Searts, age 18 and James A. Giles, age 16.
Frightened at the consequences of their
actions, the youths admitted their part in
the crime and signed statements.   James E.
Smith admitted being the man holding the
gun which went off when the female victim
grabbed it.   He had a criminal record
dating back to 1952. The four confessed
that only a few minutes before the Glessner
shooting, they had held up another man in a
parked car.

The four African-American detectives, who
had little sleep during the search for the
perpetrators, went to City Hall on Tuesday,
November 20th to be cited by the Board of
Public Safety and commended by Mayor
Philip Bayt for their outstanding work on
the case. While waiting, Detective
Lieutenant Spurgeon Davenport collapsed
and was rushed to General Hospital where
his condition was listed as fair the following
day.   He was suffering from exhaustion and
recovered.   He and Sergeants Rogers,
Glenn and Jones had been assigned to the
case by Inspector of Detectives Noel Jones.

He recommended them for citations and gave each of them two days off. [152]

June 23, 1957

Cop's Alertness Traps Attacker

153

Robert E. Butler

A shotgun wielding man terrorized three couples as they sat along the bank of Fall Creek on the north side of town, Sunday night. They were robbed and beaten. IPD Sergeant Robert Butler recalled the report of a stolen shotgun, with a Fletcher Foster,

[152] "Ace Detectives Solve Murder of U.S. Army Officer", *Indianapolis Recorder* – November 24, 1956, 1, http://indiamond6.ulib.iupui.edu/cdm/compoundobject/collection/IRecorder/id/30421/rec/1
[153] IMPD Lichtenberger History Room.

age 20 being the suspect. Upon being picked up June 28th, Foster admitted he had borrowed the gun from his brother and admitted his guilt. He was arrested and slated into court to answer on charges of robbery. [154]

July 20, 1957

35 African-American Men and Women now working for IPD

In 1957 the *Indianapolis Recorder* ran an article in their column "The Avenoo" which detailed the names and work assignments of all current African-American police officers. At this time there were 22 men and 13 women serving as sworn officers. This was an increase of only one male from 1941. Many of the women were hired in 1943 and 1951 during war time when there was a manpower shortage.[155]

---

[154] "Cop's Alertness Traps Attacker", *Indianapolis Recorder* – July 6, 1957, 1, http://indiamond6.ulib.iupui.edu/cdm/compoundobject/collection/IRecorder/id/31339/rec/1

[155] "The Avenoo", *Indianapolis Recorder* – July 20, 1957, 12, http://indiamond6.ulib.iupui.edu/cdm/compoundobject/collection/IRecorder/id/31373/rec/1

SPEEDERS BEWARE: Reported raking in traffic violators are these recent additions to the two-wheel motorcycle patrol of the Indianapolis Police Department, shown here with Capt. Audry Jacobs of the Traffic Division. Appointed during the administration of Mayor Phil Bayt and approved by Police Chief Frank Mueller, the officers Bailey Coleman (left) and William Cobb, are the first Negroes in Indianapolis Police Department history to be appointed to the 'bike patrol.' They were selected by Police Chief Frank Mueller. [156]

IPD Recruit Class Appointed February 16, 1960. African-American recruits were (front row from left) Harry Dunn, Jacqueline Winters, Joan Rayford. Third row: Robert Jackson. [157]

---

[156]   "Speeders Beware", *Indianapolis Recorder* – July 27, 1957, 1, http://indiamond6.ulib.iupui.edu/cdm/ref/collection/IRecorder/id/31388/rec/2

[157] IMPD Lichtenberger History Room.

October 23, 1957: [158]

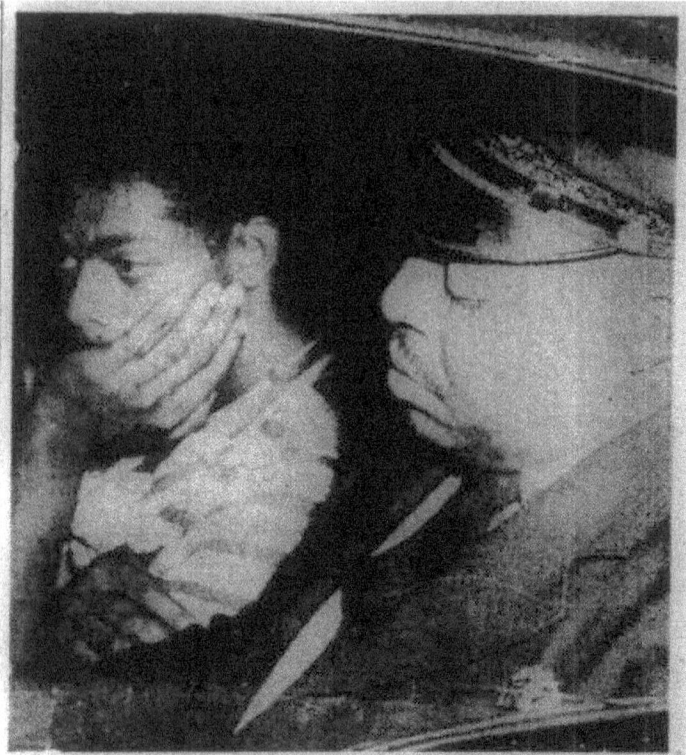

JUVENILE DELINQUENCY?: Recent teenage violence has caused many people to wonder if it can still be passed off by simply calling it "juvenile delinquency" and ignoring it. Nineteen-year-old Robert Minter is being questioned by Patrolman Warren Greene following the pistol-whipping of another youth Oct. 23. (Recorder Photo by Jim Burres)

---

[158]   "Juvenile Delinquency?", *Indianapolis Recorder* – November 2, 1957, 1
http://indiamond6.ulib.iupui.edu/cdm/ref/collection/IRecorder/id/31606/rec/16

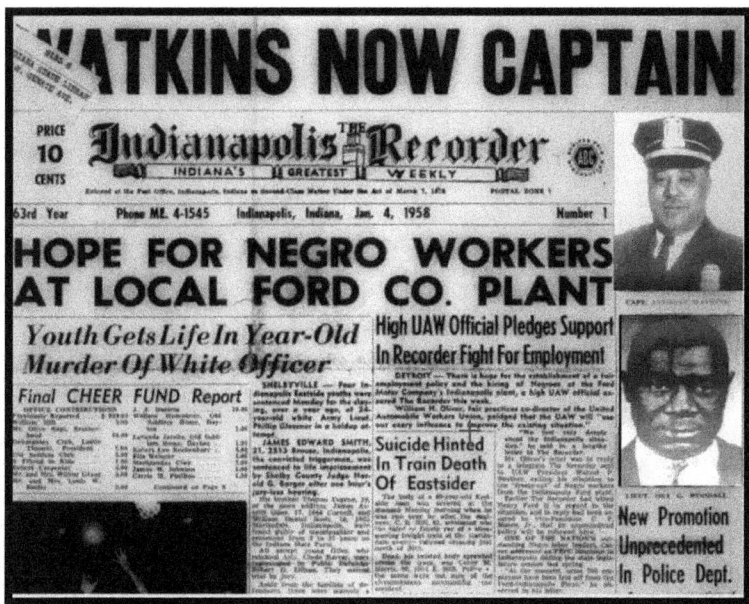

December 30, 1957

History Made: Anthony Watkins Promoted to Captain

History was made when IPD Chief of Police Frank A. Mueller recommended on December 30th the promotion of Lieutenant Anthony Watkins to the rank of Acting Captain. He is recognized as the first African-American to hold this rank with the department. Also promoted this date was Sergeant Osa Woodall, 21-year veteran, to the rank of Lieutenant in the uniform division. He had been assigned to the burglary division since 1942.[159]

July 12, 1958

Nun turned IPD Policewoman pursues resister

Maria Legg, who became a novice Catholic nun in Milwaukee, 1953, Left the nunnery and became an IPD policewoman in 1956.
On July 12, 1958 she was off duty at her apartment at 1220 N. Illinois Street when she heard a loud party in progress in

[159] "New Promotion Unprecedented in Police Dept.", *Indianapolis Recorder* – January 4, 1958, 1, http://indiamond6.ulib.iupui.edu/cdm/compoundobject/collection/IRecorder/id/31868/rec/1

Apartment 310. Going over to investigate, she opened the door, saw Mr. Dobbins in the hallway and asked him to keep it quiet. Dobbins struck at Legg with his fist and when she pulled away from
him, he grabbed her clothing.

"I showed him my badge and told him that he was under arrest, Officer Legg said. He then threw a bottle at her, inflicting a small wound on her right ring finger. Legg ran to her apartment
to get her gun, while Dobbins ran down the steps toward Capitol Avenue. As he crossed Muskingum, Officer Legg fired a shot.

Police in a patrol car heard the shot, joined in the chase and apprehended the youth as he got home. He was charged with being drunk, disorderly conduct, resisting arrest and assault and battery. He was fined $25 and sentenced to 20 days in jail.[160]

---

[160]   "Three-Block Chase Ends With Youth's Capture", *Indianapolis Recorder* – July 12, 1958, 1, http://indiamond6.ulib.iupui.edu/cdm/compoundobject/collection/IRecorder/id/32810/rec/28

August 6, 1958:

Lt. Spurgeon Davenport reads letters written by Connie Nicholas. She shot Forrest Teel and attempted to commit suicide over a failed love affair, which created a sensation in Indianapolis.[161]

---

[161]   UPI Telephoto in possession of author.

Anthony Watkins is promoted to Merit Rank of Captain

Chief of Police Recommends Officer to Board of Safety

Capt. Anthony Watkins, veteran member of the Indianapolis Police Department, was recommended by Chief Frank R. Mueller to the Board of Safety from acting to permanent captain this week. Appointed acting captain in January of this year, he was the first Negro to attain that rank in the annals of the department.

Capt. Watkins is assigned to the desk as relief desk captain. It was the first time white officers had to take orders from a Negro superior.

During an exclusive Recorder interview Watkins admitted that when he first assumed his new duties he was a little afraid some of his white fellow officers might resent having to get their orders from him.

But, the captain added, "I have had only the highest degree of respect, cooperation and help from all the men under my command and my superiors."

CAPTAIN WATKINS

Anthony Watkins promoted to Merit Captain, the week of November 22, 1958. Again, he is the first member of his race in IPD history to hold this rank, which the African-American community and the

Indianapolis Recorder had been lobbying for since the 1920's.[162]

October 1959

Ugly Incident in the South

163

IPD Policewoman Overa Ward was on vacation in a drive-in restaurant in Jacksonville, North Carolina in October 1959.   According to the North Carolina

[162] "Chief of Police Recommends Officer to Board of Public Safety", *Indianapolis Recorder* – November 22, 1958, 1, http://indiamond6.ulib.iupui.edu/cdm/compoundobject/collection/IRecorder/id/33290/rec/1
[163] IMPD Lichtenberger History Room.

authorities, Mrs. Ward claimed someone stole $20 from her at the restaurant and a disturbance ensued. Sheriff Tom Marshall claimed Patrolman Ward "flashed a badge and waved a gun in the restaurant. He confiscated her gun and badge and sent her to the home of relatives in Jacksonville, in custody of her husband. After this humiliation, he called her Chief, Robert Reilly, who said he would investigate the incident but asked that the sheriff mail her gun and badge back to IPD. [164]

---

[164] "Local Policewoman Humiliated By North Carolina Officials", *Indianapolis Recorder* – October 10, 1959, 1, http://indiamond6.ulib.iupui.edu/cdm/compoundobject/collection/IRecorder/id/38334/rec/47

February 6, 1961:

VETERAN FETES ROOKIES: Six of seven new additions to the Indianapolis Police Department were welcomed to the force in grand style recently when a high-ranking veteran officer hosted a dinner in their honor. The veteran is Captain Anthony Watkins, the first and only Negro police captain on the force. Other veteran officers were also invited to the dinner. The new officers were sworn in Jan. 31, 1961, and will take over their duties when they finish training school which is being conducted by Sgt. William Beaumont and Capt. Orville Gleich, head of the personnel bureau.

Shown in the photo above are (left to right) Sgt. James Dabner, a veteran; Joe McCoy, a rookie; Capt. Watkins; Cephus Bandy, a rookie; Paul Hooks, a rookie; Keith Vance, a rookie; Edward Lipscomb, a rookie; Paul Dean, a rookie, and Lt. Oscar Donahue, a veteran. Joseph Shelton, a rookie, was not present when photo was taken. The dinner, was held Feb. 6 in the Walker Coffee Pot.[165]

---

[165]   "Veteran Fetes Rookies", *Indianapolis Recorder* – February 11, 1961, 2,
http://indiamond6.ulib.iupui.edu/cdm/compoundobject/collection/IRecorder/id/39447/rec/2

December 10, 1961

A Step toward Integration

Roger N. Harrison

Hailed as a move toward integration within IPD, on December 10, 1961, Sergeant Roger N. Harrison was named as supervisor of Division 5, Westside. This included Squad Car No. 10 and supervising Cars 18, 21, 34, 37 and Patrol Wagon 59, all of whom were run by White officers. He had previously been in charge of Division No. 6, with cars 22 and 27, operated by African-American officers and Car 19, manned by White officers under his jurisdiction. His new jurisdiction was bounded by White River and the north, south and west city limits, including the airport.

Sergeant Harrison was quoted as saying modestly, "The Mayor, Board of Safety and Chief of Police are trying to give the people of this fine city more understanding between fellow men and a better place in which to live and have integrated the police department to show no partiality which will give greater understanding in dealing with the public." I am indeed honored to be selected as one of the first in the forward movement to make better race relations and God willing I shall strive to do my utmost not to fail Mayor Boswell, the Board of Safety and the Chief of Police Robert E. Reilly."[166]

166   "Sgt. Roger N. Harrison Named to Supervise Division 5, Westside", *Indianapolis Recorder* – December 16, 1961, 1, http://indiamond6.ulib.iupui.edu/cdm/compoundobject/collection/IRecorder/id/39968/rec/1

William Rowe (top) and Jack Yager (bottom) receive their diplomas after undergoing rigid training with their canine partners as the first African-American members of the new IPD K-9 Unit.

187

September 14, 1962

15-Year old Girl Robs Cleaning Store

The above photo depicts a 15-year old girl being led to a paddy wagon by Detective Sergeant Sam Gibbs. She allegedly had just robbed the Commerce Cleaners, 1537 Roosevelt of $37. She was said to have walked in with a .32 revolver and said, "Give me the money – all of it." She was apprehended not long afterward. [167]

---

[167] "Young Female Bandit Seized", *Indianapolis Recorder* – September 15, 1962, 2,

December 29, 1962

Promotion Board Integrated

With the addition of Captain Anthony Watkins, the IPD promotion board became integrated for the first time. L-R: Inspector Daniel Veza, Captain Charles Caine, Captain Watkins, Captain Fred Swego and Captain Joseph Hunt. [168]

---

http://indiamond6.ulib.iupui.edu/cdm/compoundobject/collection/IRecorder/id/40814/rec/1

[168] "Promotion Board Meets", *Indianapolis Recorder* – December 29, 1962, 8,
http://indiamond6.ulib.iupui.edu/cdm/compoundobject/collection/IRecorder/id/41053/rec/1

March 16, 1963

Spurgeon Davenport Given the Judge Jerome Frank Memorial Award

Spurgeon Davenport

In 1955, a man named Herbert Cross Jr. was identified by a gas station attendant as robbing Huddleston's Service Station, 5709 W. Washington Street. Lt. Spurgeon Davenport refused to believe Cross was guilty because he knew him from previous investigations. The attendant also gave the suspect's license plate number to police, which came back to a Donald O. Thomas, not Cross. Thomas was later arrested and admitted to several larcenies, but not the Huddleston Service Station robbery. Thomas spent 1955-1959 in prison.

Lt. Davenport worked during this time in trying to clear Herbert Cross, who was serving a 10-25 year sentence himself for the Huddleston robbery. In 1959, Thomas was paroled and later arrested and this time, he confessed for the Huddleston robbery.

Cross was released after spending 5 years in prison. New York University awarded Spurgeon Davenport the Judge Jerome Frank Memorial Award which honors "law enforcement officers who have shown conspicuous respect for the civil rights of persons who have become involved with the law." Davenport received a scroll and $500.00.[169]

---

[169] "Gets High Award For Clearing Innocent Man", *Indianapolis Recorder* – March 16, 1963, 1,
http://indiamond6.ulib.iupui.edu/cdm/compoundobject/collection/IRecorder/id/41224/rec/1

May 25, 1963:

170

The recruit class appointed February 16, 1963 had a record 12 African-American officers. Several of these officers reached command rank within the department and made history. In the photograph above, Front Row, L-R: Richard Crenshaw; Richard Jeter and William Myers. Back Row, L-R: Lawrence Hoskins, Richard Combs, John V. Martin; Donald Floyd; John E. Offutt; James E. Dailey and Robert C. Green. Not pictured are Melvin L. Brown and Mrs. Rosemary Simpson. A total of 42 rookies graduated.

---

[170] Photograph from Societe de Police Facebook Group.

Above from top left: Crenshaw, Jeter, Myers, Floyd, Hoskins, Dailey.

From top left: Combs, McMartin, Offutt, Green & Simpson.

October 1963

Lt. Spurgeon Davenport named to head IPD Homicide Division

Lieutenant Spurgeon Davenport was named the head of the Homicide Division. He had worked in it since its creation in 1948 and had been second in command since 1955. He is the first African-American to head any division within the Indianapolis Police Department. [171]

---

[171] "The Avenoo", *Indianapolis Recorder* - October 5, 1963, 12,

April 25, 1964

Two African-American Officers Promoted

Joe C. Berry   Thomas Bryant

Two African-American officers were elevated on April 22, 1964 by Chief Noel Jones. Sergeant Thomas Bryant, appointed in 1949, was promoted to Lieutenant and Joe C. Berry was promoted to the rank of Sergeant. They were among a total of 10 promotions made that date. Lieutenant Bryant had become a Detective Sergeant on January 1, 1959.[172]

---

http://indiamond6.ulib.iupui.edu/cdm/compoundobject/collect
ion/IRecorder/id/41695/rec/1
[172] "Two Negroes included among 11 new police promotions", *Indianapolis Recorder* – April 25, 1964, 1,

August 21, 1964: [173]

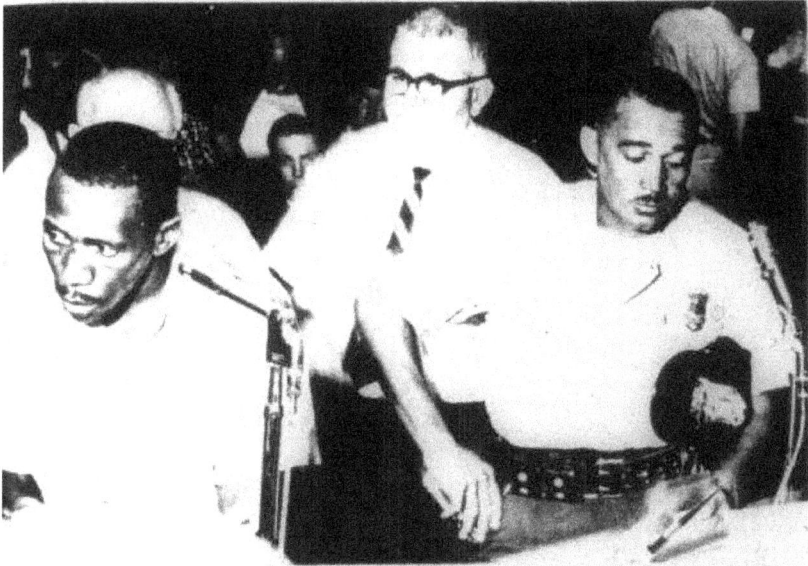

SUSPECT IN COURT: Harvey Blow (left) appeared in Municipal Court 4 Saturday after he struggled with Patralman Cicero C. Mukes (right) over possession of a gun. The officer had caught Blow, 26, running from the Jasper Engine and Transmission Exchange, 702 N. Illinois, early last Friday morning. When he returned the theft suspect to his car and attempted to handcuff him, Blow grabbed his service revolver and the scuffle began. Blow, charged with larceny, is scheduled to reappear in court Aug. 27. Bond was set at $6,000. (Recorder photo by Jim Burres)

http://indiamond6.ulib.iupui.edu/cdm/compoundobject/collection/IRecorder/id/42160/rec/1

[173] "Suspect in Court", *Indianapolis Recorder* – August 29, 1964, 1,
http://indiamond6.ulib.iupui.edu/cdm/compoundobject/collection/IRecorder/id/42466/rec/1

February 5, 1966

Spurgeon Davenport Promoted to Captain

During the week of February 5, 1966, 32-year veteran Lieutenant Spurgeon Davenport was promoted to the rank of Captain. Although he was the second member of his race to reach this rank in IPD history, it had been 8 years since the first one (Anthony Watkins in 1958). He was shifted to become head of the burglary and larceny division. Recently promoted Lieutenant Thomas Bryant was selected to replace him as head of the Homicide Division.[174]

---

[174] "Davenport Promoted to Captain", *Indianapolis Recorder* - February 5, 1966, 1,

January 7, 1967:

SUPPORT GROWING FOR DAVENPORT TO FILL NEW DEPUTY CHIEF VACANCY

On January 3, 1967, Mayor John J. Barton appointed Spurgeon Davenport to the rank of Inspector (only four such positions existed within IPD and no African-American had ever held this rank). This met with an objection by Chief of Police Noel A. Jones, who was fired by the Mayor.[175]

September 30, 1967:

L-R; Officers John Chandler and Thomas C. Watson, September 30, 1967. The two officers were one of many integrated teams assigned to high crime areas. Watson was then a rookie. [176]

---

[175] "Growing Support for Davenport to Fill New Deputy Chief Vacancy", *Indianapolis Recorder* - January 7, 1967, 1, http://indiamond6.ulib.iupui.edu/cdm/compoundobject/collection/IRecorder/id/44460/rec/1
[176] "Getting Acquainted", *Indianapolis Recorder* – September 30, 1967, 1,

February 23, 1968

Spurgeon Davenport Promoted to Deputy Chief

On February 23, 1968, Inspector Spurgeon Davenport was appointed Deputy Chief of Inspection & Training, the first African-American to hold this rank with the Indianapolis Police Department. He was the highest ranking African-American on IPD. By October of 1968, Davenport had been assigned as Deputy Chief of the

---

Investigations Division[177], putting him over Homicide & Robbery once again, which was where he well suited.

November 1968

IPD Promotes Two African-American Women to Sergeant

Thelma Sansbury   Thelma Graves

In a first for African-Americans female officers at the Indianapolis Police Department, two veteran policewomen were promoted to the rank of Sergeant on the same date. They were Thelma Sansbury, appointed in 1947, who spent much of her career in the Juvenile Aid Division and Thelma Graves, appointed in 1943, who had

---

[177]   Indianapolis Police Department Monthly Slate October-November 1968

spent years working the downtown shoplift detail. Of the 14 policewomen then serving IPD, it is believed these are the only two who held the rank of Sergeant. See their biographies for detailed information on their careers. [178]

January 1969:

A group of about 30 African-American IPD officers met and filed a list of grievances against the department, charging racial discrimination. They formed a grievance committee which included Lieutenant Chester Coates, Sergeant Paul R. Hooks and Patrolman Willie Larkins. They also formed a fact-finding committee consisting of Patrolmen Richard R. Crenshaw, John V. Martin and Tommie A. Terrell.

Among their charges was that no African-American officers were assigned to the executive branch, including the Crime Lab, logistics branch, Planning & Research and other administrative offices. They charged discrimination in the promotional process as

---

[178]   *Indianapolis Recorder* – November 16, 1968, 4, http://indiamond6.ulib.iupui.edu/cdm/compoundobject/collection/IRecorder/id/47850/rec/4

well as the hiring process. No African-Americans had a rank higher than patrolman in the Traffic Division, none were assigned to patrol cars which handled accidents. Finally, the department's African-Americans who did street duty are restricted only to the inner-city area, bounded roughly by White River to Rural Street from west to east, south of Fall Creek. The Department category denied the charges contained in the grievance. [179]

Guardians organizer Richard Crenshaw of IPD. March 1969.

---

[179] "Police dept. bias charges made by Negro personnel", *Indianapolis Recorder* – January 11, 1969, 1, http://indiamond6.ulib.iupui.edu/cdm/compoundobject/collect ion/IRecorder/id/48083/rec/1

October 26, 1969

Officer Lyman Battle earns Medal of Valor

On October 26, 1969, Officer Lyman Battle was dispatched to the 2200 block of Riverside East Drive on a serious multi-car accident. A Mercury Comet was stopped when it was rear ended by a drag racer at 80 MPH, the gas tank rupturing. When he arrived, Officer Battle found that four vehicles were involved, one of which was on fire. He went to the car and removed a man, lying him down. Returning to the vehicle, he was knocked off his feet by an explosion, which burned the soles of his

shoes off and gave Officer Battle minor
burns.

AUTO IS "COFFIN" FOR EIGHT An Indianapolis policeman
peers into a charred auto in which eight persons perished
after it was struck while unloading children at a church
by another car which was drag racing, police said. Six of
of the eight dead were children.

Lyman Battle at left.

He had already stopped the driver of one of
the drag racers, who was fleeing down the
road, his clothes in flames and wrapped him
in a blanket to extinguish the flames.
There were 13 people all together in the
burning car, including six members of one
family and three of another, all of whom

died. Four others escaped before it was hit yet again by the other speeding dragster. With the help of Deputy Chief Raymond Strattan, Officer Battle began removing people from the other three cars, one being wrapped around a tree.

He removed the charred bodies from the burning vehicle as ambulance attendants and other onlookers were too sickened to do so. This was later attributed to Officer Battle being formerly employed as a medical technician at General Hospital. Officer Battle was the first African-American to be awarded the Valor Award, the highest award the Indianapolis Police Department had.

He was also believed to be the first officer to receive five awards for the same action, including Officer of the Month for December and a certificate of commendation. His actions were described as "a credit to the department", having a "high regard for human life" and "upholding the aims and traditions of the department."[180]

---

[180] "Black officer cited for valiant efforts", *Indianapolis Recorder* - December 13, 1969, .1,

1970:

181

In 1970, Officer Ruth (Corbitt) Beaver transferred into the I.P.D. Narcotics Branch.

On June 7, 1970, the Indianapolis Star ran an article profiling the IPD Narcotics Squad, led by Sergeant Cicero C. Mukes as they made two raids and arrested multiple suspects on June 4, joining the policemen on

http://indiamond6.ulib.iupui.edu/cdm/compoundobject/collect
ion/IRecorder/id/49329/rec/1
181 IMPD Lichtenberger History Room.

these busts was Detective Ruth A. Corbitt, policewoman.

The second raid, which took place at 11:45 p.m. at 2422 Hovey Street, occurred when Det. Corbitt knocked on the door to gain entry, with Sgt. Goeden and Detective Brenton by her side.

Police recovered over 100 capsules of heroin, marijuana, hashish, a loaded .32 revolver and arrested several suspects. This is the earliest example of an undercover policewoman with the rank of Detective, on the Indianapolis Police Department.

Ruth Beaver was commended for her work in the Narcotics Branch in 1976. She resigned from IPD in 1979 to join the Drug Enforcement Agency, eventually becoming Special Agent in Charge, supervising drug operations in three states.

Ruth Beaver receives unit commendation, 1976 from Mayor Hudnut.

December 30, 1972:

IPD Officers Assist with Social Organization "The Group"

IPD officers sponsored a contest where Nettie Scott was crowned "Bahama Queen" and received a trip to the Bahama islands. Pictured are (front row) Officers R.C. Green, Robert Oatts, Thomas Tucker, James A. Smith and (second row) Tommie Terrell, James Toler, James L. Johnson, Richard Crenshaw, Harry Gurnell, James Brooks.[182]

---

[182] "The Group", *Indianapolis Recorder* – December 30, 1972, 5,
http://indiamond6.ulib.iupui.edu/cdm/compoundobject/collection/IRecorder/id/52497/rec/1

January 10, 1973

A Victim's Daughter thanks the officers who solved the case

Janet Hayes thanks Detectives John R.
Larkins (left) and James Highbaugh

The date was January 10, 1973 and the
location was the office of Deputy Chief
Ralph F. Lumpkin. The occasion was the
opportunity for a murder victim's daughter
to show her gratitude to the 16 IPD officers
who helped solve the brutal murder of her
mother. Lucile G. Hosmer, age 75 and her
husband George, age 78, had returned to

her home at 3656 N. Delaware Street the night of Friday, January 5, 1973 after attending a party. They surprised three burglars at their home. Lucile was shot to death. Her husband was wounded but survived.

By the early morning of Sunday, January 7th, IPD detectives had identified and arrested three suspects who later admitted to the murder. They were Ennis Adams, 17, Larry Cade, 18 and Walter Banks, 18. This resolution was due to 36 hours of hard detective work by members of the Indianapolis Police Department.

On January 10th, the daughter of Lucile Hosmer, Janet Gray Hayes, a member of the San Jose, California City Council arrived in Deputy Chief Lumpkin's office, where 16 men of the department were standing at attention.

"You men have done an outstanding job" she said before making a short speech to them. Then with tears in her eyes, she slowly went down the line of men, thanking each one of them. Among the four lead detectives who she spent more time with

were Detectives John R. Larkins and James
Highbaugh. [183]

March 25, 1973:

The "crack homicide team" of Detective
Sergeant Harry Dunn and Detectives James
Wyatt, James Johnson and James
Highbaugh arrest Patterson for murder on
March 25th of Armaund W. Perry. He had
been a bouncer at the Chuck-A-Luck tavern,
1435 Commerce. Within 90 minutes after
questioning patrons of the tavern, the team
made two suspects on first degree murder
charges. Arrested were Henry A.
Merriweather, age 22 and Albert B.
Patterson Jr., 22.[184]

---

[183] *The Indianapolis Star* – January 11, 1973, clipping in
possession of author.
[184] "2 Charged after tavern bouncer slain", *Indianapolis
Recorder* – March 31, 1973, 1, 15,
http://indiamond6.ulib.iupui.edu/cdm/compoundobject/collect
ion/IRecorder/id/51976/rec/1

May 3, 1973:

May 3, 1973 was declared "Jesse Owens Day" in Indianapolis by Mayor Richard G. Lugar. The 1936 Olympic champion (left) was honored during the ceremony, which was attended by Deputy Chief Spurgeon Davenport (right) and retired Captain Anthony Watkins (not pictured).

October 22, 1973

James V. Dabner Appointed Deputy Chief

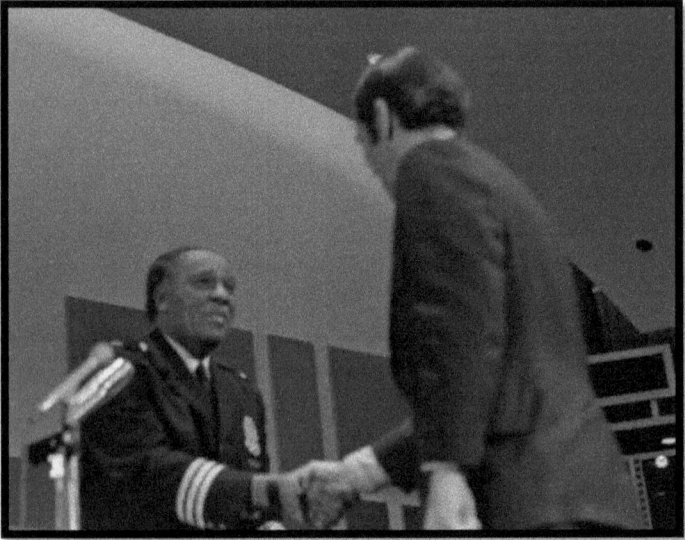

James V. Dabner was appointed Deputy Chief, replacing the retiring Spurgeon Davenport.   He was the second African-American to hold this high rank.   He assumed the position formerly held by Davenport, in charge of the Inspection and Training Division.   Earlier in his career, he and Spurgeon Davenport spent more than 11 years as an effective investigative team working out of the Homicide Division.

Dabner is pictured here with Mayor Richard G. Lugar.[185] [186]

February 2, 1974

A Murder Solved

On January 19, 1974, Robert E. Leslie, age 47, was murdered with a shotgun in his back yard.   During the following two weeks, Detective Sergeant Harry C. Dunn and Detective James Highbaugh, of Homicide, questioned more than 50 teens in the area of 40th Street and College Avenue. They had some old clothes left behind at the crime scene.   They eventually linked the clothes to Jesse D. Strong, 17. A sawed off shotgun, believed to be the murder weapon, was recovered from the Strong home ceiling. Strong admitted murdering Leslie after an argument. [187]

---

[185]   Photograph taken March 15, 1974, The Digital Mayoral Archives Collections. University of Indianapolis Digital Mayoral Archives, accessed 4/11/2014, http://uindy.archivestree.com/collections

[186]   "Dabner to succeed Davenport in police deputy chief post", *Indianapolis Recorder* – October 27, 1973, 1, http://indiamond6.ulib.iupui.edu/cdm/compoundobject/collection/IRecorder/id/53364/rec/1

[187]   "Police Seek to try youth, 17, as an adult", *Indianapolis Recorder* – February 9, 1974, 1,

April 3, 1974:

Lieutenant John Offutt became the first African-American to head the IPD Narcotics Branch.

217

October 6, 1974

IPD Stops Rape-Robbery Spree

Clockwise from top left: Richard Combs,
James Wyatt, Joseph Shelton

Indianapolis saw one of its most violent
nights in many years on Sunday, October 6,
1974. It started at 8:35 p.m. at the Hook
Drug Store, 6105 N. Keystone Avenue.
Three young men armed with a sawed-off
shotgun robbed the drug store. Before they

left, they raped an 18-year old female clerk at gunpoint.   At 10:14 p.m. three men who met the description of the Hook Drug Store robbery invaded the Linder's Ice Cream Store located at 925 Broad Ripple Avenue. They robbed the customers as well as the store and again, forcibly raped a 20-year old woman at gunpoint before leaving.

These men next visited a Taco Bell restaurant at 4390 N. Keystone Avenue. There, they robbed the restaurant and engaged in extended terrorism of the employees and customers, trying to force a customer to rape a 17-year old employee, who refused. They hit him with a shotgun, then used the gun to molest the employee.

The Indianapolis Police Department, realizing these men were dangerous to the public, assigned six detectives to the case. These men were Lieutenant Reed Moistner, head of the Robbery Detail, Sergeants Joseph Shelton, Richard Combs, James Wyatt and Detectives Joseph Lackey and James Highbaugh. The IPD team of detectives received a tip at 3 p.m., Wednesday. This led them to make rapid arrests of Alfred Rogers age 20, Charles

Murphy 14, Kevin Murphy 15 and Jeffrey
Stewart, 17 on October 9, 1974.[188]

December 21, 1974

Dunn and Lackey Capture Killer of Officer Ronald H. Manley

Officer Ronald Manley

On December 12, 1974, IPD Patrolman
Ronald H. Manley interrupted a robbery of
a Hook Drug Store at 1744 N. Illinois
Street.   They two suspects were ordered to
drop their weapons by Manley but one of

---

[188]   "Arrest 4 in Robbery, Rape, Spree", *Indianapolis Recorder*
– October 12, 1974, 1,
http://indiamond6.ulib.iupui.edu/cdm/compoundobject/collect
ion/IRecorder/id/13377/rec/1

them fired a .357 magnum, striking Manley in the head. At the same time, Manley shot one of them, identified as Robbie Allen Woods, in the chest. Both men later died at the hospital.

Scene of the murder.

The remaining suspect in the case, Norman H. Woodford, age 21, escaped. He was also suspected in the fatal shooting of a grocery store owner in Birmingham, Alabama, November 1974. Woodford was the subject of a city-wide manhunt since the murder of Officer Manley.

Directed to lead field operations in the
search for Manley's killer were Sgt. Lou
Christ and Detectives John Larkins (above)
and Jerry Campbell. They were in charge of
18 two-men teams of uniformed officers.

At 6:55 p.m., after a day long search,
Detective Sergeant Harry C. Dunn and
Detective Joseph Lackey captured Woodford
in the 300 block of N. Sherman Drive.
As Woodford was being questioned,
Detective John Larkins, Detective Sergeant
Harry Dunn and Detective Joseph Lackey
went to the 200 block of West North Street.

This was the home of a man they had learned had harbored Norman Woodford immediately after the murder of Ronald Manley. The detectives raided the home and arrested the man for being an accessory to murder.

Norman H. Woodford was given a life sentence in 1976. He was paroled in December 2003.[189] [190]

[189] "2 Others Held in murder of policeman", *Indianapolis Recorder* – December 21, 1974, 1, http://indiamond6.ulib.iupui.edu/cdm/compoundobject/collection/IRecorder/id/2094/rec/1

[190] Indianapolis Metropolitan Police Department Webpage, photo of officer, accessed April 9, 2014, http://www.indy.gov/eGov/City/DPS/IMPD/About/Memoriam/Pages/rmanley.aspx

December 20, 1975

Officer Warren E. Greene Killed in the Line of Duty

Warren Greene [191]

Officer Warren E. Greene was dispatched December 20, 1975 to a disturbance call at 324 W. 26th Street at 4:12 p.m. With him was Officer Ronald McClain, a rookie. Clifford Howard was shot by his Uncle John G. Howard with a .38 revolver. When the

---

[191] ODMP Remembers internet site:
http://www.odmp.org/officer/5715-officer-warren-edward-reene
accessed May 11, 2014

officers arrived, they found Clifford Howard lying in a pool of blood. Directing Officer McClain to return to the squad car and call for an ambulance, Officer Greene started to administer first aid.

Warren Greene checked for a pulse as John G. Howard came out of a hiding place. Officer Charles Kaiser arrived on the scene and heard Officer Greene telling John G. Howard to put the gun down. Kaiser heard shots and saw Officer Greene fall before he could assist him.

Officer Kaiser fired his revolver 6 times, knocking Howard down. As he reloaded, Officer Ernest Todd arrived on the scene. While covered by Officer Todd, Officer Kaiser started to administer first aid to Officer Greene. Officer Todd went to John Howard who although down, was still holding his weapon. Howard pointed it at Todd, who fired one shot, striking Howard in the head, killing him.

Officer Greene was transported to Wishard Memorial hospital, where he died of two gunshot wounds to the chest. Clifford Howard also died. During his funeral services, IPD Sergeant Jacqueline Winters sang two heartfelt solos. Officer Warren Greene was buried in Washington Park North Cemetery. [192]

January 1976

African-American Police Upset about Recent Appointments

Harry C. Dunn in Homicide[193]

---

[192] Indianapolis Metropolitan Police Department Webpage, photo of officer, *The Indianapolis Star*, December 21, 22 and 25, 1974, accessed April 9, 2014, http://www.indy.gov/eGov/City/DPS/IMPD/About/Memoriam/Pages/wgreene.aspx

[193] IMPD Lichtenberger History Room.

The front-page headline story on the *Indianapolis Recorder* of January 10, 1976 was titled "Black Cops 'Hoppin' Mad' at Lack of Appointments." They were upset specifically because in the first weeks of newly elected Mayor William G. Hudnut III, only one African-American had been appointed to an important post (James V. Dabner, who was retained from the previous administration as Deputy Chief of Inspection and Training.) Over 30 Black officers had called or visited the offices of the *Recorder* to complain about the situation.

One pointed complaint made by a complaining officer referred to Acting Lieutenant Harry C. Dunn being passed over for promotion to permanent head of the Homicide & Robbery Branch. "If (Chief Eugene) Gallagher was making his appointments on the basis of "hardline investigative experience" there is no way he could have passed over Dunn to head homicide and robbery," one of Dunn's coworkers in that office remarked. "You know, I know and Gallagher knows that Dunn is the best damn homicide and robbery investigator in the whole department and there are no two ways about it," the detective commented. The Homicide vacancy was created when Lt. Jack L. Cottey was appointed Deputy Chief of Investigations by Chief Eugene Gallagher.[194]

March 16, 1976

Detective James Compton Killed in the Line of Duty

Answering complaints from administrators of Crispus Attucks High School about a man

---

[194]   "Black Cops 'Hoppin' Mad' at lack of appointments", *Indianapolis Recorder* – January 10, 1976, 1, http://indiamond6.ulib.iupui.edu/cdm/compoundobject/collect ion/IRecorder/id/6806/rec/1

named Del Anthony Boatright selling marijuana to students, a team of IPD Narcotics detectives went to his house at 2145 Gent Avenue on March 16, 1976 to serve a warrant.   He was thought to be there with two other men.   Detective James M. Compton Jr., aged 29, had been assigned to the Narcotics Division for 6 weeks.

At 10 p.m. Detective Compton knocked on the door of the Gent Street address and announced that he was a police officer and had a warrant.   A shotgun was fired through the screen door.   Compton was struck in the head and chest. Falling to the ground he crawled to the middle of the front yard.   He was administered first aid by another officer while the other two detectives of the team returned fire, striking Boatright.

Both Detective Compton and Del Boatright were sent to Wishard Hospital, where the suspect died at 11 p.m.   James Compton died about an hour later.   Compton was a Vietnam veteran who was wounded in action, 1967.   He had been appointed to the Indianapolis Police Department on

February 1, 1976, after serving as a police officer for two years in the state of Kansas. He was buried in New Crown Cemetery.[195]

February 1, 1977

Larkins "Surprised" about murder probe appointment

Rated as one of IPD's top detectives, Willie Larkins was selected to join a handpicked team of detectives employed by the United States House Select Committee on Assassinations. He was in Washington D.C. for a 2 year stay for the investigation. Larkins, who received numerous citations and an F.B.I. commendation during his 12-year career, was recommended to the House Select Committee by his IPD superiors. He said he would review FBI reports on the assassinations of JFK and Dr. Martin Luther King Jr.[196]

---

[195]   Indianapolis Metropolitan Police Department Webpage, which used source of Source: *The Indianapolis Star*, March 17, 18, 20, 1976; Indianapolis News, March 19, 1976, photo of officer, accessed April 9, 2014, http://www.indy.gov/eGov/City/DPS/IMPD/About/Memoriam/Pages/jcompton.aspx

[196]   "Larkins 'Surprised' about murder probe appointment", *Indianapolis Recorder* – February 5, 1977, 2,

May 14, 1977

Detectives Harry Dunn & Joseph Lackey Solve Heiress Murder Case

Marjorie Jackson   Sgt. Harry Dunn

Marjorie Jackson was the widow of Chester Jackson, who built a chain of Standard Grocery stores in Indianapolis. When he died in 1970, she was left an estate valued at $14 million. She lived at 6490 Spring Mill Road and as the years went by, she became a recluse. In 1976 an employee at Indiana National Bank, where most of her money was deposited, embezzled $700,000 from her account. This triggered her to start making mass cash withdrawals, totaling $500,000 to $1,000,000, carrying it home in a suitcase. She squirreled this money away in closets and vacuum bags. In May of 1976, she cashed out her entire account of $9 million. She may have had a total of $11 million in her home by 1977.

Rumors started swirling about the crazy lady with the cash in her home and two young burglars, Walter Bergin Jr. and Douglas Howard Green, found numerous jewels and then came across $817,000 in cash in a closet. On May 1, 1977, thieves broke into Marjorie Jackson's home and made off with $1,000,000 in cash.

On May 2, 1977, Howard Willard and Manuel Lee Robinson robbed Jackson of $160,000. Two nights later they returned and surprising Mrs. Jackson, she was shot and killed with a .22 in her kitchen. The men tried to cover up the crime by setting fire to the house but did a poor job of it. The home was set back from the road and it took a few days for the damage to be noticed.

On May 7th, firemen found the body and called for police. IPD found over $5 million in cash, most of it stuffed in a 32-gallon trash can. Two IPD Homicide detectives, Sergeant Harry Dunn and Detective Joe Lackey, got a tip on May 6, 1977, that Manuel E. Robinson was spending money in a "big way" around 22nd and Talbot Street.

Thus, Detective Sergeant Dunn was aware of what was going on even before the discovery of the body. [197] Several people were eventually arrested for the Jackson murder, including Howard "Billy Joe" Willard and Manuel Lee Robinson. Willard was convicted of murder and died in prison serving a life sentence. Robinson, convicted of burglary and arson, was paroled in 1988. Police recovered $3.3 million of the stolen money. [198] This was said to be the largest

---

[197] "Two black detectives solve case", *Indianapolis Recorder* – May 14, 1977, 1, http://indiamond6.ulib.iupui.edu/cdm/compoundobject/collection/IRecorder/id/22460/rec/1

[198] *The Indianapolis Star* – May 2, 2013 "Retro Indy", retrieved May 18, 2014, http://www.indystar.com/picture-gallery/news/history/retroindy/2014/04/29/retro-indy-the-marjorie-jackson-murder/8452957/

robbery in United States history at the time.

November 14, 1977

Dunn and Lackey Solve a Murder – Without being assigned to it

Mr. Congelosi, a northwest-side restaurant manager, was murdered on November 6, 1977. He was ordered by the robbers to lie on the kitchen floor of the restaurant. While reaching for his wallet, the victim was shot in the head. The solution to the case came unexpectedly. Both Detective Sergeant Harry C. Dunn and Detective Joseph Lackey worked off-duty as security guards at a bank branch at 38th and Sherman Drive. On November 11th, while working there, they saw two men pull into the lot and pull a "flim-flam" trick of putting an old television set in a new box and sell it to a stranger as a brand new set. The detectives had seen these two men together numerous times. They broadcast the plate number, finding it went to a rental vehicle.

Two days later, the Congelosi murder case was assigned to two White detectives. While in the Homicide office on November 14th, Harry Dunn glanced at the murder case's teletype report and noticed the suspect's description and their car matched the ones they had seen at the bank parking lot.

At this time, the two flim-flam men were back at the lot trying to pull another rip-off. Detective Lackey was at the bank working part time and called Sergeant Dunn with this information. After being informed of their resemblance to the murder suspects, Detective Lackey arrested both of them.[199]

[199] "2 solve case without even being assigned", *Indianapolis Recorder* – November 19, 1977, 1,
http://indiamond6.ulib.iupui.edu/cdm/compoundobject/collect
ion/IRecorder/id/23001/rec/1

November 6, 1979

Officer Gerald Griffin Killed in the Line of Duty

Gerald Griffin   Cicero Mukes

On November 6, 1979, IPD Officer Gerald Griffin answered a domestic call at 4702 W. 36th Street. As he walked into a carport, he encountered Richard Moore, the male half of the domestic, who fired a shotgun at Griffin, fatally wounding him. Detective Joe Lackey was one of the first on the scene, finding Officer Griffin's body. Lackey ordered the SWAT team out. As the incident progressed, Officer Roy Potter and Lieutenant Cicero Mukes were also shot.

Mukes was hit in the face and was in serious condition at Wishard Hospital.

The suspect was Richard Moore, who had murdered his wife and her father prior to shooting Officer Griffin. SWAT and the Indiana State Police wounded Moore twice in the chest. He was captured and survived to receive a death sentence, but died in 2006 before it could be carried out.[200]

January 1981

Joseph Shelton promoted to Assistant Chief

Mayor William G. Hudnut appointed Joseph J. Shelton, a 19-year veteran of IPD to the position of Assistant Chief, in January 1981. This was at that time the highest rank attained by an African-American within the department. "I am proud to be the recipient of this high honor", Shelton told an applauding audience at a reception at the St. Peter Claver Center, held

---

[200] "Black police lieut. among 4 wounded", *Indianapolis Recorder* – November 10, 1979, 1,
http://indiamond6.ulib.iupui.edu/cdm/compoundobject/collection/IRecorder/id/21938/rec/1

January 24, 1981 to recognize his achievement. Mayor Hudnut said "Joe Shelton earned his promotion through dedication and hard work. I am proud of his promotion and am extremely happy to be able to honor Joe today." [201]

August 3, 1981: Officer Gwendolyn Black receives an ward for bravery from Mayor William H. Hudnut. Officer Black was involved in a gun battle March 6, 1981 with a suspected armed robber, which ended

---

[201] "400 at reception welcoming Joe Shelton as Police Department's Assistant Chief", *Indianapolis Recorder* – January 31, 1981, 7, http://indiamond6.ulib.iupui.edu/cdm/compoundobject/collection/IRecorder/id/25556/rec/1

with his arrest without injury. Sergeant
Michael Schmitt (in plain clothes), assisted
in the arrest.   Chief of Police Joseph G.
McAtee at left.

Bank Robbery – August 28, 1981

Policewoman holds shotgun as holdup loot and robber's gun lie in street; Deputy John Kass returns to patrol car

Policewoman Dianna Ferguson-Mosley
holds a shotgun on bank robbers as they are
searched by fellow officers on the east side.

May 15, 1982

Policewoman Earns Medal of Bravery

On November 3, 1981, Officers Michael Fay and Gloria West took a run of a fight in progress at 608 Terrace Avenue. Fay entered the apartment and someone closed and locked the door behind him. Then three men began beating him and were trying to get his gun. Officer West reached the front door and saw him being kicked.

Without hesitation, West crashed through the glass door bodily and waded into the fight. "I just slugged the first sucker that came at me. Hit him right in the jaw. The adrenalin was pumping and all I was thinking was another police officer needed help. There wasn't nothing that was gonna keep me out."

Gloria West received several lacerations and glass fragments in both eyes. Other officers arrived to assist in subduing the suspects. One of them kicked West as he was pushed in the paddy wagon. She stood at the curb bleeding and shook glass from her hair, while looking to see if she had broken any fingernails.

Officer West was awarded in May 1982 the Medal of Bravery. "I guess I've always been a fighter – both physically and mentally. I'm not afraid of anyone." [202]

[202]   "Policewoman earns medal of bravery", *Indianapolis Recorder* – May 15, 1982, 1,
http://indiamond6.ulib.iupui.edu/cdm/compoundobject/collection/IRecorder/id/28162/rec/1

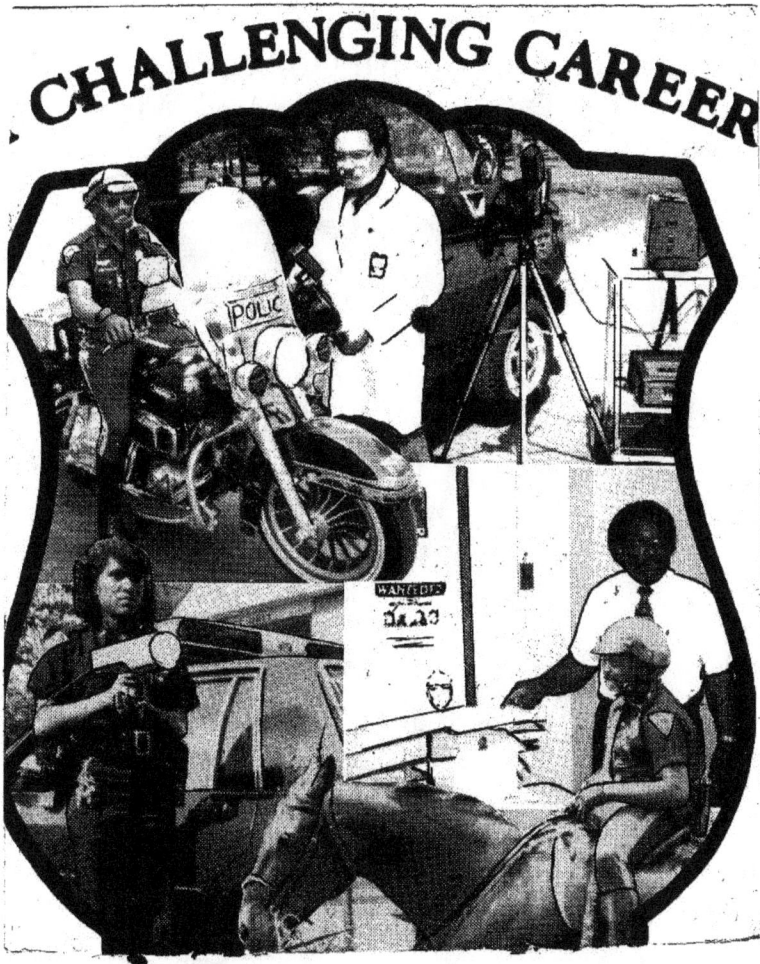

Minority Recruiting Poster, about 1983-84.[203]

---

[203] Courtesy Joseph Fishback.

Mayor William Hudnut on July 9, 1983 at Black Expo. Top: With Officers Steve Odle and LeEtta Davenport. Bottom: With Officer Deborah Saunders.

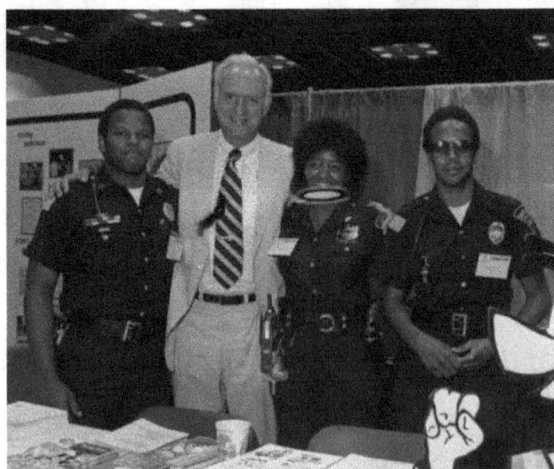

April 16, 1986

Two African-American officers achieve a first for IPD

Deborah Saunders   Robert Allen

On April 16, 1986, two African-American officers were promoted and achieved a first for their race or sex. Sergeant Deborah Saunders was promoted to the rank of Lieutenant. She was the first African-American woman with IPD to hold this rank. She was assigned to a field command. Also on this date, Robert G. Allen was promoted to Captain and assigned to the Traffic Division, the first

African-American to hold that rank in that division.[204] [205]

Mayor William G. Hudnut III and his command staff. L-R: Front Row: Chief of Police Paul Annee, Mayor William G. Hudnut, Assistant Chief John E. Offutt. L-R: Back Row: Deputy Chief James E. Campbell, Major Peter Bolles, Major Robert Allen, Major Robert Snow, Major James D. Toler, Major Penny Davis, Major Chris Dahlke, Deputy Chief Robert Ward, Deputy Chief Michael Fogarty.

---

[204] William Alexander, "IPD Promotes Black Woman to Lieutenant", *Indianapolis Recorder* – April 26, 1986, 2, http://indiamond6.ulib.iupui.edu/cdm/compoundobject/collect ion/IRecorder/id/47302/rec/1

[205] IMPD Photographs.

Charyl Davis was the first African-
American female Homicide investigator in
IPD history, 1980's.

January 1, 1992

James D. Toler appointed Chief of Police

On January 1, 1992, Mayor Stephen Goldsmith appointed Captain James D. Toler to be Chief of the Indianapolis Police Department.   This was a first for IPD. James D. Toler was a 32-year veteran of the department and a Vietnam veteran.   He was appointed Major in 1986 and had served in the field. [206]

---

[206]   IMPD Records.

Patricia Holman – Command Staff – August 1994

August 1994: Patricia Holman appointed to Deputy Chief of North District (First African-American female to hold this rank). 207

---

207   "Holman Seeks Consistency in IPD", *Indianapolis Recorder* – August 20, 1994, 1, http://indiamond6.ulib.iupui.edu/cdm/compoundobject/collection/IRecorder/id/74003/rec/1

<u>January 1999:</u> Chief of Police Michael Zunk appointed Deborah Saunders Assistant Chief of Support Services, making her the highest ranking African-American female in the history of the department. She had previously served as Deputy Chief of the Downtown District. [208]

---

[208] "Black recruits and rewards on the rise in IPD", *Indianapolis Recorder* – January 29, 1999, 1, 3, http://indiamond6.ulib.iupui.edu/cdm/compoundobject/collection/IRecorder/id/3140/rec/1

February 20, 2002: Patricia Holman was promoted to Captain. She was the first African-American female to hold this rank. [209]

---

[209]   IMPD Records.

June 2002

Lt. Dianne Ferguson-Mosley – Only African-American Female to head a Detective Branch

In the year 2006, Lieutenant Dianna L. Ferguson-Mosley was placed in charge of the the IPD Robbery Branch, the first female Lieutenant in IPD history to do this. She is also the first and only African-American woman had been chosen to head a branch of detectives. She later headed the Organized Crime Section, another group of detectives.[210]

---

[210]   Ibid

www.ingramcontent.com/pod-product-compliance
Lightning Source LLC
Chambersburg PA
CBHW071955040426
42447CB00009B/1337